The Agenda

How a Republican
Supreme Court Is
Reshaping America

COLUMBIA GLOBAL REPORTS
NEW YORK

The Agenda
How a Republican Supreme Court Is Reshaping America

Ian Millhiser

The Agenda:
How a Republican Supreme Court Is Reshaping America
Copyright © 2021 by Ian Millhiser

Published by Columbia Global Reports
91 Claremont Avenue, Suite 515
New York, NY 10027
globalreports.columbia.edu
facebook.com/columbiaglobalreports
@columbiaGR

Library of Congress Cataloging-in-Publication Data
Names: Millhiser, Ian, author.
Title: The Agenda: How a Republican Supreme Court is Reshaping America / Ian
    Millhiser. Description: New York, NY : Columbia Global Reports, [2021] | Includes
    bibliographical references. |
Identifiers: LCCN 2020055178 | ISBN 9781734420760 (paperback) | ISBN
    9781734420777 (ebook)
Subjects: LCSH: United States. Supreme Court. | Judges--United States--Attitudes. |
    Conservatism--United States.
Classification: LCC KF8748 .M55 2021 | DDC 347.73/26--dc23
LC record available at https://lccn.loc.gov/2020055178
Book design by Strick&Williams
Map design by Jeffrey L. Ward
Author photograph by Holley Matthews

Printed in the United States of America

CONTENTS

Introduction

From 2011, when Republicans gained control of the House of Representatives and denied President Barack Obama a governing majority, until the pandemic forced Congress's hand in 2020, Congress enacted hardly any major legislation outside of the tax law President Donald Trump signed in 2017.

In the same period, the Supreme Court dismantled much of America's campaign finance law, severely weakened the Voting Rights Act, permitted states to opt out of the Affordable Care Act's Medicaid expansion, created a new "religious liberty" doctrine permitting someone who objects to the law on religious grounds to diminish the rights of third parties, weakened laws shielding workers from sexual and racial harassment, expanded the right of employers to shunt workers with legal grievances into a privatized arbitration system, undercut public sector unions' ability to raise funds, effectively eliminated the president's recess appointment power, and halted President Obama's Clean Power Plan.

Plus, lest you think that the last decade was a never-ending stream of losses for liberals, the Court held that every state must permit same-sex couples to marry, and it held that federal anti-discrimination law prohibits employers from firing individuals because of their sexual orientation or gender identity.

The Supreme Court, in other words, has become the locus of policymaking in the United States. The lion's share of the legal changes that have occurred over the last decade were spearheaded, not by elected officials, but by the nine unelected members of the nation's highest Court.

And, with Republicans now controlling two-thirds of the seats on the Supreme Court, the Court could potentially sabotage any policy initiative pushed by President Joe Biden. It can also manipulate our voting rights laws to ensure that Republicans dominate future elections.

Part of the explanation for the shift in power from the elected branches to the judiciary is that congressional dysfunction fosters judicial dominance. As Professor Rick Hasen explains in a 2012 study, Congress is now nearly 80 percent less likely to enact legislation overriding a Supreme Court decision than it was several decades ago. Hasen defined the term "override" to include any "successful piece of federal legislation [that] overturned, reversed, or modified a Supreme Court statutory interpretation holding."

Between 1975 and 1990, Congress enacted "an average of twelve overrides of Supreme Court cases in each two-year Congressional term." That number shrunk to 5.8 overrides "for each term from 1991 to 2000, and to a mere 2.8 average number of overrides for each term from 2001 to 2012."

As Congress has grown more partisan and more polarized, Hasen explained, it's become less and less able to form the
consensus necessary to override an erroneous Supreme Court
decision. Though there are still rare cases where a single political party controls both Congress and the presidency, and the
members of that party agree that a particular Supreme Court
decision should be overruled, "partisanship seems to have
strongly diminished the opportunities for bipartisan overrides
of Supreme Court cases, in which Democrats and Republicans
come together to reverse the Supreme Court."

As Congress grows less and less able to enact ordinary legislation, the Supreme Court is more and more likely to become
the final word on questions of policy.

Hasen's study, however, only offers a partial explanation
of the Supreme Court's increasing dominance. Congress, after
all, only has the power to override court decisions interpreting
(or misinterpreting) a federal statute. When the Supreme Court
declares a law unconstitutional, that decision can only be overruled by the Supreme Court itself—or, in extraordinarily rare
instances, by a constitutional amendment.

The full story of how the Supreme Court grew into the most
important policymaking body in the United States is also a story
about partisan polarization. It is a story about how the justices—
and the men who appointed those justices—themselves became
polarized.

For much of the last several decades, Democrats and Republicans largely shared a bipartisan consensus that the courts
should play a limited role in society. Indeed, if anything, Republicans tended to be *more* skeptical of judicial power than their
Democratic counterparts. President Richard Nixon campaigned

against judges who "impose their social and political viewpoints
upon the American people." President Ronald Reagan promised
judges who would exercise "judicial restraint." President George
W. Bush warned of judges who "give in to temptation and make
law instead of interpreting."

Indeed, until very recently, conservative lawyers organized
around the principle that courts should be very cautious about
exercising too much power. In a 2006 address to the conservative Federalist Society, for example, former federal appellate
judge and then secretary of homeland security Michael Chertoff credited the society for catapulting arguments for judicial
restraint into the legal mainstream. "In large part because of the
work that the Society and others have done," Chertoff claimed,
"the claim for judicial modesty is sufficiently well-established
that everybody understands, even the critics of that claim, that
they have to take it seriously and they have to address it."

But judicial modesty is now very much out of fashion in
conservative legal circles. Many of the same men and women
who spent the second Bush administration arguing that judges
need to exercise judicial restraint are now the most vocal advocates for increased judicial power. In 2005, for example, future
justice Neil Gorsuch denounced "American liberals" who "have
become addicted to the courtroom, relying on judges and lawyers rather than elected leaders and the ballot box, as the primary
means of effecting their social agenda on everything from gay
marriage to assisted suicide to the use of vouchers for private-
school education."

And yet, as a member of the Supreme Court, Gorsuch has
called for the judiciary to claim a broad new power to veto federal regulations. He's argued that courts should give Christian

12   conservatives broad exemptions from the law. And he's even
      suggested that the Court should revive an antiquated "freedom
      of contract" doctrine that it once used to strike down basic labor
      protections such as a minimum wage.

      Indeed, Justice Gorsuch, who once accused liberals of using
      litigation to implement their policy preferences regarding pri-
      vate school vouchers, joined a Supreme Court decision forcing
      states with voucher programs to provide such vouchers to reli-
      gious schools.

      So what happened? How did a political party that, until very
      recently, was very fearful of judicial power learn to stop wor-
      rying and love judicial activism? To answer this question, we
      need to examine more than a century of Supreme Court history.

The Golden Age of Conservative Judicial Activism

"If you ask me where American aristocracy is found," Alexis de
Tocqueville wrote in *Democracy in America*, "my reply would be
that it would not be among the wealthy who have no common
link uniting them. American aristocracy is found at the bar and
on the bench." Lawyers, according to de Tocqueville, "are secretly
opposed to the instincts of democracy, their superstitious
respect for what is old; to its love of novelty; their narrow views,
to its grandiose plans; their taste for formality, to its scorn for
rules; their habit of proceeding slowly, to its impetuosity."

The law—or, at least, the law as it largely existed in the
early American republic that de Tocqueville observed—was
much less a creation of democratically elected lawmakers than
it was the slow, iterative creation of judges who, by deciding
individual cases and trying to follow earlier rules laid down in

prior precedents, developed a rich and complex "common law" over the course of hundreds of years. Much of today's law governing contracts, property, and what happens when one individual injures another owes at least as much to English common law judges who died hundreds of years ago as it does to elected officials. The lawyers and judges de Tocqueville observed saw themselves as custodians of this common law tradition, and many of them feared legislators empowered to cast aside the wisdom of a dozen generations of judges in favor of the momentary whims of the masses.

But de Tocqueville also wrote about a nation on the cusp of an economic revolution. Before the railroads, someone traveling from New York to San Francisco needed to either complete a four-month sailing voyage around the southern tip of South America, or they could risk a dangerous shortcut through Panama that often ended in death from a tropical disease. After the transcontinental railroad's completion in 1869, by contrast, it took only six days to make the same journey across the United States.

Industrialization transformed America. Before the railroads, a farmer in Iowa would most likely take their grain to a nearby market where it would be sold exclusively to other Iowans. After the railroads, the same grain would be loaded on a train to Chicago, stored in one of a handful of grain elevators where it was combined with similar grain from across the Midwest, and then shipped out via another rail line for sale in New York or Richmond or potentially even overseas.

In a pre-industrial America, local businesses served local customers, and were isolated from competition by far-off merchants. In the post-industrial America, farmers, miners,

14 and manufacturers throughout the nation all competed with each other in a single market that spanned the entire country. Small businesses risked being bigfooted by massive new corporations—or by trusts formed for the specific purpose of crushing competitors. Men like John D. Rockefeller, Andrew Carnegie, and Cornelius Vanderbilt amassed fortunes that would shame medieval kings and Roman emperors.

And this vast wealth placed legions of workers under their control in factories and worksites where men, women, and children labored with few rights and little ability to push back against oppressive bosses.

A common law developed for a largely agrarian society comprised of local, isolated economies was ill-suited for a rapidly industrializing nation. Slow, deliberative change was the hallmark of the common law. Such a legal system simply could not adapt fast enough to provide for a newly nationalized economy or the vastly different working conditions many Americans endured after industrialization.

And yet the legal profession—or, at least, the elite members of the legal profession who were most likely to become judges or Supreme Court justices—retained the conservative sensibility that de Tocqueville observed.

The United States, American Bar Association (ABA) president Edward Phelps told that organization in an 1881 address, "can endure all its other dangers with less apprehension than the action of its federal and state legislation inspires." Phelps, in a warning that was typical of the views of many elite lawyers in the early industrial era, warned that "legislatures in this country are steadily grasping larger powers, and approaching nearer and nearer to omnipotence," and that this new dominance of the people's representatives risks "the gradual extinction of those principles of civil liberty which the history of the world shows to be inseparable from the common law."

Indeed, this fear of legislative power infected many lawyers who, at least for their time, might be viewed as champions of many of the downtrodden. Moorfield Storey, another future ABA president who would go on to serve as founding president of the National Association for the Advancement of Colored People (NAACP), told the State Bar Association of New York in 1894 that "the business community throughout the nation welcomes the adjournment of Congress as the end of a season filled with perplexity and dread," and that "when a state legislature meets, every great corporation within its reach prepares for self-defense, knowing by bitter experience how hospitably attacks upon its property are received in committee and on the floor."

Arguably the most important legal scholar of the Gilded Age was a law professor named Christopher Tiedeman. Professor Tiedeman, who argued that judges should impose strict constitutional limits on lawmakers' power to regulate the workplace and the economy more generally, bragged in the second edition of one of his treatises that "the first edition of the book has been quoted by the courts with approval in hundreds of [court] cases."

Tiedeman, moreover, was unapologetic about his belief that courts should read the Constitution creatively in order to suppress democracy. "The conservative classes," Tiedeman wrote in one influential treatise, "stand in constant fear of the advent of an absolutism more tyrannical and more unreasoning than any before experienced by man—the absolutism of a democratic majority." To fight this "absolutism," Tiedeman urged

16 courts to "lay their interdict upon all legislative acts" that violated his theory of liberty, "even though these acts do not violate any specific or special provision of the Constitution."

The culmination of Tiedeman's vision was the Supreme Court's decision in *Lochner v. New York* (1905), which struck down a New York law limiting the amount of time bakery workers could be required to work to sixty hours a week and ten a day.

Lochner rested on the principle that the New York law was an "unnecessary and arbitrary interference with the right of the individual to his personal liberty or to enter into those contracts in relation to labor which may seem to him appropriate or necessary for the support of himself and his family." The idea was that, if a worker agrees to sell more than sixty hours of labor to an employer in a week, and the employer agrees to pay for that labor at a certain wage, then the state generally may not interfere with that contract.

Lochner, moreover, presumed that this freedom to contract benefited workers and employers alike. "Of course," Justice Rufus Peckham wrote for the Court, "the liberty of contract relating to labor includes both parties to it. The one has as much right to purchase as the other to sell labor." Later decisions would rely on *Lochner* to strike down minimum wage laws (on the theory that workers have the freedom to contract to be paid less than the minimum wage), and to strike down laws protecting workers' right to join a union (on the theory that employers may refuse to contract with unionized workers).

The later decision, it is worth noting, was written so broadly that it likely would have rendered any anti-discrimination law unconstitutional. "It is not within the functions of government," the Court held in *Adair v. United States* (1908), "to compel any person in the course of his business and against his will to accept or retain the personal services of another, or to compel any person, against his will, to perform personal services for another." Taken seriously, that means that a civil rights law cannot require a racist business owner to employ African Americans.

It should be said that *Lochner*'s premise that workers and employers both benefit from such a rigid "liberty of contract" was, at best, woefully naive. Around the time of *Lochner*, the average bakery employee worked between thirteen and fourteen hours a day, and some worked much longer hours—one bakery imposed a 126-hour workweek on its bakers. Because bakery workers were typically paid by the week or by the day, long hours did not yield more pay. At the turn of the twentieth century, few bakers earned more than $12 a week, or about $16,000 a year in modern-day dollars.

They often worked these long hours surrounded by filth and decay. The New York City bakeries of this era were frequently built in the basements of tenements, where sewer pipes that carried the upstairs residents' waste ran overhead. Often, these pipes would leak their contents, dripping raw sewage onto the workers and onto the very workstations where those workers prepared the dough.

"Filth, cobwebs, and vermin" abounded in these basement bakeries, according to an inspector's official report to the New York State Legislature, as did "rats and mice." In one bakery, "the water closets were literally black with cockroaches." In another, raw sewage spilled into the ferment tub holding yeast used to produce the bakery's bread. In a third, a defective sink caused waste water to fill the bakery floor, "creating pools of putrid

18   water and piles of mud, exhaling odors so vile that the desire to escape to the sidewalk became irresistible."

Often, the workers were forced not just to work, but to sleep in these conditions. In some bakeries, a worker might lay a mattress across the flour barrels so they had a place to sleep between shifts. Often, workers slept on the very same tables where they kneaded the dough—and the price of these makeshift accommodations was deducted from their wages.

So these were the conditions that the free market provided to workers in a world without government regulation. And yet, the Supreme Court of this era persisted in claiming that freedom of contract was a system that benefited worker and owner alike. As the Court said in *Adair*, "The employer and the employe [sic] have equality of right, and any legislation that disturbs that equality is an arbitrary interference with the liberty of contract which no government can legally justify in a free land."

The Age of Democracy

*Lochner*ism—and a broader sense that the Constitution prohibits a wide range of progressive policies—held sway over the Supreme Court for more than a generation. But it met its match in President Franklin Delano Roosevelt. Though the Court spent much of Roosevelt's first term striking down New Deal policies, it abandoned *Lochner* in the late 1930s and ushered in a new age of democratic governance.

It's hard to imagine an act of Congress more likely to offend *Lochner*'s defenders than the National Labor Relations Act of 1935 (NLRA). The NLRA provides that "[e]mployees shall have the right to self-organization, to form, join, or assist labor organizations, to bargain collectively through representatives of their own choosing, and to engage in other concerted activities for the purpose of collective bargaining or other mutual aid or protection." Thus, the law took direct aim at the *Lochner*ian idea that the best system for workers and employers alike is one where the government does not interfere too much with employment contracts.

Nor were the lawmakers who drafted the NLRA shy about their disdain for the Supreme Court's workplace decisions. The law states explicitly that it seeks to end the "inequality of bargaining power between employees who do not possess full freedom of association or actual liberty of contract," and many of their employers. A labor market driven by *Lochner*'s idea of freedom of contract, according to the NLRA's drafters, "tends to aggravate recurrent business depressions, by depressing wage rates and the purchasing power of wage earners in industry and by preventing the stabilization of competitive wage rates and working conditions within and between industries."

Indeed, the NLRA was doubly offensive to *Lochner* Era conservatives. Not only did it question the idea that the best way to provide for workers is a largely unchecked free market, it was also a federal law that sought to protect workers' rights throughout the nation—and the *Lochner* Era Court was especially skeptical of federal laws seeking to regulate the workplace.

In *Hammer v. Dagenhart* (1918), for example, the Supreme Court struck down a law prohibiting goods produced by child laborers from traveling across state lines or otherwise being sold in interstate commerce.

Although the Constitution permits Congress to "regulate commerce ... among the several states," *Hammer* read this power to regulate interstate commerce very narrowly. "Commerce," the

20 Supreme Court reasoned, should be defined narrowly to include the transit and sale of goods—and not the actual manufacturing of goods that will later be transported across state lines to be sold. Thus, because the purpose of the child labor law at issue in *Hammer* was to regulate who could be involved in manufacturing these goods—and not the transit or sale of the goods themselves—the law was beyond Congress's power to enact.

And yet, less than two decades after *Hammer*, the Supreme Court abandoned this narrow vision of federal power and upheld the NLRA. The manufacture of goods, the Court reasoned in *NLRB v. Jones & Laughlin Steel Corp* (1937), has "such a close and substantial relation to interstate commerce" that it makes no sense for the courts to draw a line between manufacturing and commerce. Labor strife, the Court added, can have "a most serious effect upon interstate commerce"—indeed, a large enough strike can potentially shut down such commerce altogether. So Congress should be allowed to shift the balance of power between workers and employers if it believes that doing so will reduce such strife.

A year later, in *United States v. Carolene Products* (1938), the Court laid out a comprehensive theory of when the judiciary should strike down federal or state laws—and when it should allow the democratic process to play out unmolested.

The primary thrust of *Carolene Products* is that, when the government regulates business, the workplace, or the economy more generally, courts should presume that this law is constitutional. As Justice Harlan Fiske Stone put it, in somewhat needlessly turgid prose, "regulatory legislation affecting ordinary commercial transactions" should not be struck down unless "it is of such a character as to preclude the assumption that it rests upon some rational basis within the knowledge and experience of the legislators."

In a famous footnote, Stone then listed several cases where this presumption of constitutionality could be overcome. They include laws that violate an explicit provision of the Constitution, laws that restrict "those political processes which can ordinarily be expected to bring about repeal of undesirable legislation"—such as by suppressing the votes of individuals who are likely to oppose a particular law—or laws that target a "discrete and insular" minority group.

Thus, *Carolene Products* established a strong presumption in favor of democracy—in nearly all cases, the people's democratically elected representatives should decide the nation's policy, and not unelected judges. One of the judiciary's primary roles, moreover, was to keep the wheels of democracy turning by striking down laws that tended to rig elections or cut minority groups permanently out of power.

The remarkable thing about this democratic settlement is that it held for nearly three-quarters of a century. Indeed, for most of the last half-century, Republicans were often the voices of judicial restraint, warning against liberal judges who might impose their own policy preferences upon the nation. Hence Nixon's warning against judges who "impose their social and political viewpoints upon the American people," or George W. Bush's jeremiads against judges who "give in to temptation and make law instead of interpreting."

But this era of conservative judicial restraint did not last, and even most legal experts were surprised by how quickly conservative defenders of judicial restraint lost their sway over the Republican Party during the Obama presidency. On the eve

22   of oral arguments in *NFIB v. Sebelius* (2012), the first Supreme
      Court case seeking to repeal Obamacare, an American Bar Asso-
      ciation poll of Supreme Court experts found that 85 percent
      predicted that the law would be upheld, and another 9 percent
      predicted that the Supreme Court would dismiss the case as
      premature. That left only a tiny fraction predicting that the law
      would be struck down.

      The consensus among legal experts, in other words, was that
      the Court would continue to honor the presumption in favor
      of democracy announced in *Carolene Products* and respected by
      the Supreme Court for three generations. Instead, four justices
      voted to repeal the Affordable Care Act in its entirety. And a fifth,
      Chief Justice John Roberts, initially voted to strike down sev-
      eral key provisions of the law—including the provisions pre-
      venting insurance companies from denying coverage to people
      with preexisting health conditions—before eventually changing
      his mind and voting to leave most of the law in place.

      Eight years after *NFIB*, the Supreme Court is even more
      conservative than it was on the day that Obamacare nearly died.
      Trump appointees Neil Gorsuch and Brett Kavanaugh are more
      conservative than the men they replaced. And, on many issues,
      Trump's final appointment, Amy Coney Barrett, is the polar
      opposite of Justice Ruth Bader Ginsburg, the feminist icon Bar-
      rett replaced.

      The *Carolene Products* settlement in favor of democracy is
      now in tatters.

      The death of conservative judicial restraint is not sur-
      prising. As Yale law professor Jack Balkin writes in an essay
      explaining why this shift happened, American political history
      can be "organized around a series of political regimes in which

one party is dominant and sets the agenda for political contest." Early in one party's regime, "the newly dominant party faces opposition from judges appointed by the old regime and obstacles from the constitutional jurisprudence those judges created"—and so the newly dominant party tends to embrace a rhetoric of judicial restraint.

Yet, as a party's control of the political agenda continues, it will fill more and more seats on the federal judiciary. Eventually, a long-ascendant party will gain such a dominant position in the courts that judicial restraint starts to look like unilateral disarmament. A party that controls the Supreme Court has nothing to fear from judicial activism, and everything to gain from it.

Which is not to say that every single member of a dominant political party will change their views about the proper role of the courts overnight. As Balkin explains, the effect is "generational." "[O]lder legal intellectuals may cling to their long-held beliefs about judicial review, while younger thinkers adopt a different perspective."

Thus, the best explanation for Roberts's vote in the Obamacare case is likely that he straddles a generational divide between Reagan-era conservatives—who still feared that their agenda could be thwarted by liberal judges—and Trump-era conservatives who've spent their careers wishing that a conservative judiciary would do more to implement a conservative agenda. Someone like Neil Gorsuch, by contrast, shows no inclination toward judicial restraint because he's only known one era.

Gorsuch was five years old on the day that the Supreme Court handed down *Roe v. Wade* (1973). He's spent his entire career hoping for the courts to do more, and being disappointed when they did less.

    This book explores what the six Republicans who control the Supreme Court are likely to do with their power. As Roberts's apostasy on Obamacare suggests, these six Republicans do not think entirely alike. Roughly speaking, there are at least three distinct ways of thinking within the Court's Republicans.

By far the most radical member of the Supreme Court is Justice Clarence Thomas—although it remains to be seen whether Barrett, who has not been on the Court long enough to develop much of a record, will meet or even exceed Thomas's extremism. Thomas, for example, is the only member of the Supreme Court to suggest that the Court was correct to strike down child labor laws more than a century ago.

Justice Thomas often argues that avulsive constitutional change is necessary in order to restore the "original understanding" of our founding document. Thus, Thomas tends to argue that such change is necessary because of his ideological commitment to a particular method of constitutional interpretation. (Though Justices Gorsuch and Barrett have not been on the Court long enough to fully assess their approach to the Constitution—we don't know yet how either judge approaches child labor, for example—both Gorsuch and Barrett share Thomas's broad "originalist" philosophy.)

Justice Samuel Alito, by contrast, is the closest thing the Supreme Court has to a pure Republican partisan. As of this writing, Alito is the only conservative justice who has never joined his liberal colleagues in a 5–4 decision—meaning that he's never been the deciding vote for a liberal result.

And then there's Chief Justice Roberts, whose occasional departures from conservative orthodoxy were a subject of great fascination while Roberts controlled the median vote on

the Supreme Court. But that brief moment when Roberts was
both the chief justice and the swing justice is now over, thanks
to the confirmation of Justice Amy Coney Barrett. Republicans no longer need Roberts's vote to prevail. (Kavanaugh, like
Barrett, has not been on the Court long enough to fully assess
his approach to the law. While Kavanaugh sometimes engages
in textualist rhetoric similar to Gorsuch's, he also sometimes
behaves more like Roberts or Alito.)

Moreover, while Roberts does sometimes recoil from the
massive legal shifts advocated by men like Gorsuch or Justice Clarence Thomas, Roberts is hardly a paragon of judicial restraint himself. It was Roberts, after all, who wrote the
Supreme Court's decision in *Shelby County v. Holder* (2013),
which dismantled much of the Voting Rights Act. And it was
Roberts who wrote opinions like *McCutcheon v. Federal Election
Commission* (2014), dismantling much of our laws regulating
campaign finance.

Roberts rejects a wholesale return to *Lochner*. But his
record suggests that he is eager to implement bold conservative changes that will fundamentally transform the relationship
between American voters and their government. And, if more
justices in the vein of Gorsuch or Kavanaugh are appointed to
the Supreme Court, it is very possible that the Supreme Court
of the near future will look much like the *Lochner* Era Court.

So what does America's legal future look like? And what
will the Supreme Court's current majority do with the power it
now holds?

This book hones in on several areas where we can be fairly
confident that at least five members of the current Court will
support significant rightward shifts in the law—regardless of

whether the justices in the majority are driven by originalist ideology, Republican partisanship, or something else.

The first chapter of this book dives into the single most important topic in any free nation: voting rights. More than a century ago, the Supreme Court acknowledged that the right to vote is "preservative of all rights." Formal legal rights mean little if our leaders are not accountable to the people.

And yet, the Roberts Court has been unusually hostile to voting rights. In *Crawford v. Marion County* (2008), it all but eliminated a rule prohibiting laws that impose restrictions on the right to vote that vastly exceed the benefits of that law. In *Shelby County*, the Court effectively struck down a key provision of the Voting Rights Act, which required states and localities with a history of racial voter suppression to "preclear" any new voting laws with officials in Washington, D.C. And in *Abbott v. Perez* (2018), the Court held that victims of intentional racial voter discrimination must overcome such a high burden of proof that it may no longer be possible for such plaintiffs to prevail in all but the most egregious cases.

All of this has happened while the Court was simultaneously undercutting our regulation of campaign finance, permitting partisan gerrymandering to go unchecked, and defunding much of the Democratic Party's political infrastructure. And all of these prior decisions could only be the tip of the iceberg. Now that the relatively moderate Justice Anthony Kennedy is no longer around to provide a check on the Court's Republican majority, much more of our law protecting the right to vote is likely to fall.

And it's worth noting that Republicans on the Supreme Court are able to launch such an attack on voting rights solely because our constitutional system rejects the basic democratic principle that all votes should count equally. Donald Trump, after all, lost the popular vote to Hillary Clinton by nearly three million ballots in 2016. And at present, the Senate is malapportioned to effectively give extra seats to votes from conservative, largely white states.

The first justice in American history to be nominated by a president who lost the popular vote and confirmed by a bloc of senators who represent less than half the country is Trump's first appointee, Neil Gorsuch. The second is Brett Kavanaugh, Trump's second appointee. And the third is Amy Coney Barrett, Trump's third.

Chapter Two will discuss one of the least understood, and most important, areas of American law—the power of the federal administrative state. Many federal laws lay out a broad policy seeking to improve access to health care, reduce pollution, prevent exploitation of workers, or to achieve any of a myriad of other goals. The details of implementing this policy are then delegated to policy experts within an agency like the Environmental Protection Agency or the Department of Health and Human Services.

Beginning in the Obama administration, however, the Republican Party's top legal minds turned sharply against such delegations of power to Executive Branch agencies. Annual gatherings of the Federalist Society, which played an outsized role in selecting President Trump's judicial appointees, became showcases for various proposals to strip federal agencies of their ability to regulate business. Hostility toward federal agency power became an "unspoken litmus test" for anyone hoping to be appointed to the Supreme Court during the Trump presidency.

28   Five members of the Court's Republican majority, meanwhile, have signaled that they intend to give themselves a broad
new veto power over federal agencies. The practical impact of
such a decision will be that future presidents and their subordi-
nates will need to seek permission from a conservative judiciary
to implement all sorts of policy changes.

Chapter Three turns to the subject of religion. Until very
recently, the Court struck a careful balance between protecting
religious liberty and maintaining the rule of law in a plural-
istic society. Religious people enjoyed a robust right to practice
their own faith, but they could not wield religious liberty claims
to cut away the legal rights of others. This was especially true
in the business context. As the Supreme Court held in *United
States v. Lee* (1982), "[w]hen followers of a particular sect enter
into commercial activity as a matter of choice, the limits they
accept on their own conduct as a matter of conscience and faith
are not to be superimposed on the statutory schemes which are
binding on others in that activity."

But the Court held for the first time, in *Burwell v. Hobby
Lobby* (2014), that religious objectors may invoke their faith
to limit the rights of a third party. Now that this wall's been
breached, the Court is likely to give religious conservatives a
broad new power to defy laws that they object to on religious
grounds—including, most likely, the power to ignore many
anti-discrimination laws.

Yet, even as the Court's shown extreme solicitude for the
grievances of conservative Christians, it's been far less sympathetic to religious liberty claims brought by adherents to
less politically powerful faiths. Hence the Court's decision to

uphold President Trump's travel ban imposed on several largely
Muslim nations.

Chapter Four will then consider a threshold question facing
anyone who hopes to vindicate their legal rights in court—who
is allowed to sue in the first place? The Roberts Court has given
major corporations sweeping power to immunize themselves
from class action lawsuits, and an even broader power to shunt
workers and consumers into a privatized arbitration system that
tends to favor corporate parties. These, and other similar decisions, risk turning basic legal rights into paper tigers. After all,
what's the point of a law prohibiting workplace discrimination
or forbidding wage theft if workers cannot sue to enforce it?

There is a unifying theme surrounding these four chap-
ters. This Court has, at times, protected controversial rights,
including the right to an abortion and the right to be free from
anti-LGBTQ discrimination—although the right to an abortion
is unlikely to survive much longer. But the four topics explored
by this book—democracy, administrative law, religion, and the
right to sue—all involve cases that extend far beyond any individual right and that shape the very nature of our government.

There is little doubt that, if Republicans maintain their current majority on the Supreme Court, the law will lurch hard to
the right on issues like abortion, affirmative action, and private
school vouchers. But the purpose of this book is not to itemize
every policy change that's likely to be implemented by a Republican Court. Rather, it's to examine Supreme Court decisions that
cut across all issue areas. A Republican Supreme Court will fundamentally alter the structure of the American system of government, and who is allowed to exercise power within that system.

The cases discussed in this book concern fundamental questions such as: Who is actually allowed to make use of their legal rights? Who is beyond the reach of the law? How is the government allowed to address the many complex problems facing a modern state? And they concern the most important question of all: Who chooses the people who make our laws?

A right to be free from discrimination means nothing if it cannot be enforced in court. Or if the person engaged in discrimination is above the law. Or if lawmakers elected by a small, conservative segment of the population can repeal that right.

If you take one lesson from this book, it should be this: The Supreme Court operates in subtle ways. The full impact of its decisions rarely can be gleaned from the cases that draw the biggest headlines or that are most comprehensible to non-lawyers. And some of the Court's least understood and most arcane decisions are fundamentally reshaping our nation—transforming it into something far less democratic.

The danger presented by a 6–3 Republican Court, in other words, is far greater than a decision tossing out *Roe v. Wade*. The current Supreme Court is likely to build a nation where conservatives, and only conservatives, have the opportunity to govern.

The Right to Vote

In 2013, North Carolina's Republican legislature enacted what voting rights advocates soon labeled the state's "monster" voter suppression law. As a federal appeals court opinion striking down this law explained, "The General Assembly enacted legislation that restricted voting and registration in five different ways, all of which disproportionately affected African Americans."

This disproportionate impact on Black voters, moreover, was not a coincidence. Before enacting the law, state lawmakers "requested data on the use, by race, of a number of voting practices." It then used this data to shape many of the details of the law, ensuring that it would discourage thousands of African Americans from casting a ballot, while having a much smaller impact on white voters.

The North Carolina law, for example, did not simply require voters to show photo ID at the polls—a highly dubious practice because voter ID laws target a problem, in-person voter fraud at

32   the polls, that is virtually nonexistent. Rather, the North Carolina law also prohibited voters from using certain forms of
government-issued identification, including "student IDs, government employee IDs, public assistance IDs, and expired IDs"
for voters under the age of seventy, to cast a ballot. Why were
these particular forms of ID excluded? As the appeals court
explained, the law permitted "only those types of photo ID disproportionately held by whites and excluded those disproportionately held by African Americans."

Similarly, the racial data that the state legislature relied on
to draft this law "revealed that African Americans disproportionately used early voting in both 2008 and 2012"—in 2012,
over 64 percent of African Americans voted early, compared
to less than half of whites. Black voters were especially likely
to vote in the first seven days of early voting. So the "monster" law eliminated these seven days. That also eliminated
one of the two Sunday voting days when Black churches often
held "souls-to-the-polls" events that bus parishioners to early
voting places.

The timing of the North Carolina law, moreover, was not
a coincidence. Republican governor Pat McCrory signed this
law in August of 2013, less than two months after the Supreme
Court's decision in *Shelby County v. Holder* weakened the Voting
Rights Act and enabled North Carolina to change its voting
laws without federal supervision. Indeed, a Republican leader
announced plans to enact an "omnibus" election law on the very
next day that *Shelby County* was decided.

The North Carolina law is a particularly aggressive example
of a phenomenon that is very common in states with large
African American populations and Republican legislatures—

partisan preferences tend to be racially polarized, and Black voters are especially likely to prefer Democrats to Republicans. In 2016, for example, CNN exit polls found that 63 percent of white voters in North Carolina preferred Republican Donald Trump to Democrat Hillary Clinton, while a massive 89 percent of Black voters preferred Clinton to Trump.

If Republicans enact a law that effectively disenfranchises thousands of African Americans, that law will shift the overall electorate toward the GOP. In a close election—and North Carolina's 2016 race for the governor's mansion was decided by fewer than five thousand votes—such laws can determine who wins and who loses.

Although early data suggests that Trump performed better among voters of color in 2020 than he did in 2016, NBC exit polls still show Democratic president Joe Biden winning 87 percent of Black voters and 65 percent of Latinos. Laws that disenfranchise many communities of color will disproportionately target Democrats.

The Supreme Court is almost entirely polarized along partisan lines regarding whether to protect voting rights from laws such as the one enacted in North Carolina. *Shelby County*, after all, was a 5–4 decision, with all five of the Court's Republican appointees in the majority, and all four Democrats in dissent.

Indeed, it is likely that, had Justice Antonin Scalia's death not deprived Republicans of a majority on the Supreme Court for most of 2016, the North Carolina election law would have been in effect during that year's election. All four of the Court's Republicans voted to reinstate nearly all of the law in 2016, despite the appeals court's determination that the law targets "African Americans with almost surgical precision."

34   The Republican majority on the Supreme Court will likely continue to hand down decisions undercutting voting rights. Indeed, it has already dismantled much of the legal framework that propped up such rights for most of the last half century.

The Four Crumbling Pillars of American Voting Rights Law
Before Chief Justice Roberts took over his role as the nation's top jurist, four pillars supported the right to vote. Under Roberts's leadership, however, the Court has dismantled two of these pillars and severely weakened a third. And it is likely that the Court now has the votes to destroy the fourth.

In *Crawford v. Marion County Election Board,* the Court rejected a challenge to Indiana's voter ID law. Defenders of such laws often argue that they are necessary to prevent fraudsters from impersonating someone else at the polls, but numerous studies and investigations have determined that such fraud is an almost entirely imaginary problem.

A study by Loyola Law School professor Justin Levitt, who led much of the Justice Department's voting rights work during the Obama administration, found just thirty-five credible allegations of in-person voter fraud among the 834 million ballots cast in the 2000–2014 elections. A Wisconsin study found seven cases of fraud among the three million cast in the 2004 election, none of which were the kind that could be prevented by a requirement to show photo ID at the polls. Iowa Republican secretary of state Matt Schultz concluded a two-year investigation into election misconduct within his state in 2014. He found zero cases of voter impersonation at the polls.

Notably, the lead opinion in *Crawford* was only able to identify a single case of in-person voter fraud in the previous 140 years.

Meanwhile, many studies suggest that voter ID laws disproportionately disenfranchise groups such as students, low-income voters, and voters of color—all of whom tend to prefer Democrats over Republicans. Admittedly, the studies examining the impact of voter ID are all over the map. At least one found no meaningful impact on turnout. Others found that they can skew an election toward Republicans by three points or more. In 2012, data journalist Nate Silver estimated that a Pennsylvania voter ID law would have reduced "President Obama's margin against Mitt Romney by a net of 1.2 percentage points" if it had taken effect.

So, at best, voter ID laws inconvenience voters without having a measurable impact on elections. At worst, they potentially shift the electorate toward Republicans by a larger margin than Biden's margin over Trump in many crucial states. And there is no evidence at all that such laws accomplish anything worthwhile.

And yet, the Court allowed Indiana's law to take effect. Even more significantly, the Court's decision in *Crawford* effectively removed a safety valve the Supreme Court previously used to weed out laws that impair the franchise, in order to target an illusionary problem.

One challenge that arises in voting rights cases is that the government must have some power to regulate elections. It must be able to determine where voters should cast their ballots, for example, or what those ballots should look like, or what date absentee ballots must be mailed by in order to be counted.

On the margins, these laws can disenfranchise some voters. If a state law requires a mailed-in ballot to be postmarked by November 3, and a voter forgets to drop it in the mail until

36 November 4, that voter's ballot will not be counted. Nevertheless, the Constitution does and should tolerate such marginal incursions on the right to vote. It would be impossible to administer an election without some constraints on the times, places, and manner that voters cast their ballots.

At the same time, there also must be constraints on the states themselves, to prevent them from enacting election procedures that seek to skew elections. A state must not be allowed to, for example, provide significantly more voting machines to polling places in white neighborhoods than it does in Black neighborhoods with similar populations. It should not have an excessively complicated voter registration process, where many voters are disenfranchised because of a minor error on a registration form that is difficult to fill out properly. And it should not impose ID requirements on voters that serve no actual purpose.

Thus, as the Supreme Court held in *Burdick v. Takushi* (1992), courts must be vigilant against voting restrictions that impose significant burdens on voters, without providing much benefit in return. "A court considering a challenge to a state election law must weigh 'the character and magnitude of the asserted injury'" to the right to vote against "'the precise interests put forward by the State as justifications for the burden imposed by its rule,' taking into consideration 'the extent to which those interests make it necessary to burden the plaintiff's rights.'"

Under this framework, voter ID laws cannot be justified, as they impose a burden upon voters without advancing any legitimate purpose. Though *Burdick* has not been explicitly overruled, *Crawford* permits states to enact at least some voter restrictions that advance no goal other than potentially skewing the electorate toward the GOP.

The second major pillar of America's voting rights framework was the preclearance regime struck down in *Shelby County*. Under that regime, states and localities with a history of racial voter suppression had to submit proposed changes to their election laws and procedures either to the Department of Justice or a federal court in Washington, D.C. And the proposed change would not be approved if it had "the purpose [or] . . . the effect of denying or abridging the right to vote on account of race or color."

A key feature of this provision of the Voting Rights Act was that it required federal officials to screen out racial discrimination *before* a new voting law took effect. Courts are not especially agile institutions, and it often takes years for voting rights lawyers to build the case against a voter suppression law, present their evidence to a court, obtain a court order striking down that law, and then litigate that case through a maze of appeals.

In the Jim Crow era, this meant that southern states could lock African Americans out of the polls by enacting one voter suppression law, running one or more elections under that law, and then enacting a new—sometimes only slightly different—law once the courts finally got around to striking the first one down. In the modern era, this problem still persists in many contexts. A perennial problem in racial gerrymandering cases, for example, is that states frequently run two, three, or even four elections under a map that is ultimately struck down.

That means that lawmakers have a profound incentive to enact gerrymanders and other forms of voter suppression, even if those laws will ultimately be invalidated by a court order. If the state gets to run just one rigged election under the invalid law, the lawmakers behind that law will benefit from it.

The immediate impact of the Voting Rights Act, with its provision halting many voter suppression laws before they could take effect, was profound. On the day President Lyndon Johnson signed this act into law, just 7 percent of Mississippi's eligible Black voters were registered to vote. After only two years under the Voting Rights Act, this number rose to nearly 60 percent.

Many Republicans recognized immediately that they'd been given a gift when the Supreme Court invalidated the preclearance regime in *Shelby County*. As noted above, North Carolina Republicans announced their plans to enact an omnibus law making it harder to vote in that state on the day after *Shelby County* was decided. Texas announced that its voter ID law and its racially gerrymandered legislative maps would go into effect just two hours after *Shelby County* was decided.

Chief Justice Roberts's majority opinion in *Shelby County* is a tribute to wishful thinking. The premise of that opinion is that, while the United States was once tainted by the kind of "'pervasive,' 'flagrant,' 'widespread,' and 'rampant' discrimination" that can justify an extraordinary federal law requiring states to seek permission from federal officials before they can change their only election rules, that time has passed. "[T]hings have changed dramatically," Roberts wrote. America, at least according to Roberts and his four Republican colleagues, simply isn't racist enough anymore to justify the "strong medicine" imposed by the Voting Right Act's preclearance regime.

Just three years later, the United States made Donald Trump its president. Numerous empirical studies have shown that "racial resentment" drove a significant segment of voters who backed Trump.

Roberts, for what it's worth, was right about one thing in *Shelby County*. Trump's election aside, America in the twenty-first century does not resemble the Jim Crow South. African Americans do vote in large numbers throughout the country. Laws such as voter ID seek to reduce Black turnout around the margins, not prevent African Americans from voting entirely. Many Black politicians serve in Congress. Barack Obama served two terms in the White House.

Things have changed dramatically. But they changed because America enacted laws to ensure that those changes would happen. As Justice Ruth Bader Ginsburg wrote in her *Shelby County* dissent, "Throwing out preclearance when it has worked and is continuing to work to stop discriminatory changes is like throwing away your umbrella in a rainstorm because you are not getting wet."

Shelby County, it should be noted, left much of the Voting Rights Act intact. Among other things, it did not touch a provision that forbids any state law that "results in a denial or abridgement of the right of any citizen of the United States to vote on account of race or color." This provision is less potent than the preclearance regime, because it does not block voter suppression laws before they take effect—it requires voting rights lawyers to file lawsuits and obtain actual court orders in order to stop such laws—but it still offers some protection against racial voter suppression.

Except that the Supreme Court has begun to chip away at what remains of the Voting Rights Act as well. And it is likely to cut so deeply into the Voting Rights Act's protections against voter suppression that America's most important voting rights law could become a paper tiger.

If you want to understand why the Voting Rights Act is such an important law, even in a nation that has made such significant racial progress since the days of the Jim Crow South, recall the fact that African Americans are one of the most reliably Democratic constituencies in the nation. The 2018 exit polls show that 90 percent of Black voters chose a Democratic candidate for the US House, while only 9 percent voted for a Republican. So lawmakers who wish to inflate the likelihood that Republicans will prevail in a future election can be pretty sure that they are reducing the Democratic Party's vote share if they enact a law that targets Black voters.

These lawmakers may not be motivated by white supremacy. They may not have any philosophical opposition to allowing Black people to vote simply because of the color of their skin. But they target African Americans nonetheless because they want to prevent *Democrats* from casting a ballot.

After *Shelby County*, the Voting Rights Act still permits victims of racial voter discrimination to prevail in two instances: if a law was enacted with racist *intent* or if the law leads to a racially discriminatory *result*, even if lawmakers didn't necessary intend such a result. These two remaining prongs of the Voting Rights Act—the "intent" test and the "results" test—are two of the major pillars of America's voting rights regime.

Except that, in *Abbott v. Perez* (2018), the Supreme Court placed such a high burden on plaintiffs attempting to prove racial intent that it is far from clear that this burden can be met outside of truly egregious cases.

The facts of *Perez* are, to say the least, complicated. In 2011, the Texas state legislature drew new congressional maps, some parts of which were eventually stuck down as illegal racial gerrymanders. The full 2011 map never took effect, however, due to a federal court's decision that it did not comply with the pre-*Shelby County* version of the Voting Rights Act.

That placed Texas in a bit of a bind. Without a lawful map that it could use to conduct its 2012 elections, the state might not have been able to conduct congressional elections at all. As a stopgap measure to ensure that the state could still have an election, a Texas federal court held that Texas could conduct its 2012 election using a hastily drawn interim map that left in place two congressional districts that were later determined to be illegal racial gerrymanders. Yet this federal court was also careful to warn Texas that, in giving the state permission to use these stopgap maps for a single election, it wasn't relieving Texas of its obligation to draw legal maps in the future. "This interim map," the court told Texas, "is not a final ruling on the merits of any claims asserted by the Plaintiffs in this case or any of the other cases consolidated with this case."

Nevertheless, Texas's Republican-controlled legislature decided that it liked these interim maps so much that it would make them permanent. In 2013, the governor called a special legislative session to repeal the 2011 maps and replace them with the interim maps—which, again, were in many relevant respects identical to the 2011 maps. *Perez* asked whether, by reenacting the exact same racially gerrymandered districts, but under somewhat different circumstances a couple of years later, Texas somehow cleansed those districts of the racist intent that initially motivated the state legislature to draw them in a particular way.

The thrust of Justice Samuel Alito's majority opinion in *Perez* is that state lawmakers accused of acting with racist

42   intent enjoy an extraordinarily high presumption of racial innocence. "Whenever a challenger claims that a state law was enacted with discriminatory intent, the burden of proof lies with the challenger, not the State," Alito wrote. And this "rule takes on special significance in districting cases."

Just how high is this burden of proof? According to Alito, "the only direct evidence brought to our attention suggests that the 2013 Legislature's intent was legitimate. It wanted to bring the litigation about the State's districting plans to an end as expeditiously as possible." That, the Supreme Court held in *Perez*, was enough to cleanse the 2013 maps of the racist intent that motivated the (again, identical in all relevant respects) 2011 maps.

The Supreme Court, in other words, held that the 2013 maps weren't enacted to preserve a racial gerrymander; they were enacted to shut down litigation challenging a racial gerrymander. And, somehow, that distinction was enough to defeat the plaintiffs' claim in *Perez*.

If the Supreme Court is this willing to ascribe innocent motives to lawmakers accused of acting with racist intent, it should go without saying that voting rights plaintiffs will struggle to win *any* case alleging intentional racial discrimination. Absent overwhelming evidence such as the kind of cartoonishly racist statements normally associated with figures like George Wallace, cases alleging racist intent are likely to be doomed. And even if a voting rights plaintiff does have such evidence at hand, lawmakers may still be able to rescue a racist law by reenacting it, and claiming that the sole purpose to the reenactment is to shut down the lawsuit attempting to get that law struck down.

And that brings us to the final pillar of America's voting rights regime, the Voting Rights Act's "results" test. Under this test, a voting rights plaintiff does not need to prove that a particular law was enacted with racist intent. They merely need to show that it has the effect of making it harder for voters of a particular race to cast a ballot.

At the moment, the results test still stands. But it is very likely that there are five votes on the current Supreme Court to declare it unconstitutional. Indeed, Chief Justice Roberts, the most moderate member of the Court's Republican majority, has been a vocal opponent of the results test since the early 1980s. And the Supreme Court has already agreed to hear a case in its 2020–21 term that it could use to weaken, or even destroy outright, the results test.

The Future of Voting Rights
Under a Republican Supreme Court

To understand what the future of voting rights is likely to look like, we have to first go back four decades, to the Supreme Court's decision in *City of Mobile v. Bolden* (1980). In that case, the Court upheld Mobile, Alabama's practice of electing each of its city commissioners at-large by the city as a whole—despite the fact that this allowed the city's white majority to vote as a bloc to prevent any Black candidate from becoming a commissioner.

Mobile established, albeit only briefly, that voting rights plaintiffs must show that a law was enacted with a "racially discriminatory motivation" in order to challenge that law.

Two years after *Mobile*, however, Congress overwhelmingly approved an amendment to the Voting Rights Act that established the modern-day results test. And President Ronald Reagan

44   signed this bill into law. But he did so over the strenuous objec-
      tion of a young Justice Department attorney named John Roberts.
          Shortly after completing his clerkship for conservative
      justice William Rehnquist, Roberts joined a cadre of polit-
      ical appointees within DOJ who were determined to roll back
      many of the legal victories civil rights attorneys had achieved
      over the previous two decades. "This is an exciting time to be
      at the Justice Department," Roberts wrote at the time to Judge
      Henry Friendly, a prominent appeals court judge that Roberts
      also clerked for. The future chief justice added that he found his
      new employer to be such an exciting place to work because "so
      much that has been taken for granted for so long is being seri-
      ously reconsidered."
          According to voting rights journalist Ari Berman, Rob-
      erts became the Reagan administration's point person in its
      failed effort to preserve the narrow reading of the Voting Rights
      Act embraced in the *Mobile* decision. "Roberts wrote upwards
      of twenty-five memos opposing an effects test for Section 2,"
      according to Berman. The future chief "drafted talking points,
      speeches, and op-eds for [Attorney General William French]
      Smith and [Assistant Attorney General William Bradford]
      Reynolds; prepared administration officials for their testi-
      mony before the Senate; attended weekly strategy sessions; and
      worked closely with like-minded senators on Capitol Hill."
          Many of the arguments Roberts raised against the amended
      Voting Rights Act track the arguments he would later use to
      nullify preclearance. *Shelby County* is, at its heart, a states' rights
      opinion. Preclearance, Roberts writes in the first paragraph
      of that opinion, "required States to obtain federal permission
      before enacting any law related to voting—a drastic departure

from basic principles of federalism." Similarly, the younger John
Roberts wrote in a memo arguing against the results test that
expanding the Voting Rights Act would "provide a basis for the
most intrusive interference imaginable by federal courts into
state and local processes."

Indeed, Roberts suggested at times that the proposed
amendment to the Voting Rights Act would violate the Constitution itself, arguing in a 1982 memo that the results test "would
establish essentially a quota system for electoral politics."

Arguably the single most toxic word in race discrimination
cases is the word "quota." This is the word Justice Lewis Powell
used in *Regents of the University of California v. Bakke*, when he
struck down a medical school's affirmative action program that
ensured that at least 16 percent of the student body would be
people of color. Ever since *Bakke*, racial conservatives have used
the word "quota" when they wish to suggest that a program
intended to combat racial injustice is unconstitutional.

Admittedly, Roberts compared the modern-day Voting
Rights Act to a racial quota system nearly forty years ago. And
he did so while he was still a junior lawyer working on behalf of
his conservative bosses. But there is good reason to believe that
Roberts's views have not changed since he became chief justice.

In 2014, the Supreme Court heard *Texas Department of
Housing and Community Affairs v. Inclusive Communities Project*,
a case asking whether the federal Fair Housing Act functions
much like the Voting Rights Act's results test. *Inclusive Communities* asked whether the Fair Housing Act permits "disparate
impact" lawsuits—that is, suits claiming that a housing policy
is illegal because it has a "disproportionately adverse effect on
minorities." In a 5–4 decision authored by now-retired justice

Anthony Kennedy, the Court concluded that the Fair Housing Act does permit such lawsuits.

Though both Kennedy's majority opinion and the principal dissent in *Inclusive Communities* turned largely on a disagreement about how to read the text of the Fair Housing Act, Roberts strongly implied at oral argument that he believes that disparate impact lawsuits are unconstitutional because they lead to a racial quota system.

One of Roberts's core beliefs is that all laws that explicitly take account of race are equally odious, regardless of whether they were enacted to preserve white supremacy or to tear down racial separation. As the chief justice wrote in an opinion claiming that two public school districts violated the Constitution when they enacted race-conscious policies designed to desegregate their schools, "The way to stop discrimination on the basis of race is to stop discriminating on the basis of race."

When Roberts looked at the Fair Housing Act—and at the possibility that it permits disparate impact lawsuits— he saw a similar problem. "Is there a way to avoid a disparate impact consequence without taking race into account in carrying out the governmental activity?" Roberts asked, during the *Inclusive Communities* oral argument. He then added that "it seems to me that if the objection is that there aren't a sufficient number of minorities in a particular [housing] project, you have to look at the race until you get whatever you regard as the right target."

The chief justice, in other words, appears to view any law that seeks to root out state laws or policies that have a discriminatory impact on racial minorities as unconstitutional. And

Roberts is typically the most moderate member of the Supreme Court's Republican majority.

So it is very likely that there are now five votes on the Supreme Court to strike down the Voting Rights Act's results test. And with it, any meaningful checks on race discrimination in state election laws. So what does the world look like without real checks on racial voter discrimination? The short answer is that laws like the one we saw in North Carolina are probably only the beginning.

Consider Alabama. In 2015, after a strict voter ID law went into effect in that state, Republican governor Robert Bentley announced plans to close thirty-one government offices that issue driver's licenses—most of them in rural, low-income, majority-Black counties. At the time, an esti-mated 250,000 Alabamans lacked the ID required to vote, so this plan to close so many of the offices where people obtain such ID could have potentially disenfranchised thousands of African Americans.

Bentley largely backed down from this plan to shut down so many driver's license offices, after an Obama administration probe determined that this plan violated a federal civil rights law, but that was before Justice Kennedy left the Court. Without Kennedy, it is far from clear that there are still five justices who believe that the government may ban conduct that has a dispa-rate impact on voters of color.

Or consider Texas. Very early in the morning on March 4, 2020—after polls were already closed in most of the state and Texas's high-stakes Democratic presidential primary had already been called for Joe Biden—Hervis Rogers cast a ballot in a polling place located at a historically Black college in Houston.

48   Rogers was the last person in line. He'd waited six hours and twenty minutes to vote.

And Rogers was just one of countless voters in heavily Democratic Houston who had to endure long waits in order to cast a ballot.

Rogers's long wait, moreover, was not an isolated incident. Between 2012 and 2018, Texas closed 750 polling places. And these closures appeared to target voters of color, while largely sparing white Republicans. According to the *Guardian*'s Richard Salame, "the fifty counties that gained the most Black and Latinx residents between 2012 and 2018 closed 542 polling sites, compared to just thirty-four closures in the fifty counties that have gained the fewest Black and Latinx residents."

If you want a vision of what the future will look like if the Supreme Court dismantles what remains of America's voting rights infrastructure, look to places like Texas and Alabama. At least on the surface, this future will look very different from Jim Crow. Voters of color will still be permitted to cast a ballot, for the most part, and many of them still will.

But Republican-controlled states will also be able to use race as a proxy to identify voters who are likely to vote for Democrats. And they will be able to erect special obstacles that make it much harder for these voters to cast their ballots. In a nation closely divided between Democrats and Republicans, that could be enough to lock in Republican control of many states and, as more and more states fall, to lock in Republican control of Congress.

A Final Note About Gerrymandering

Thus far, this chapter has focused on one of the most consequential changes the Supreme Court's current majority is

likely to make to America's election law—effectively dismantling what remains of our safeguards against racial voter discrimination. As of yet, Chief Justice Roberts's decades-long
crusade against the Voting Rights Act remains incomplete.
He still needs to wait for an appropriate case, and to convince
four of his fellow Republicans to join him, if he hopes to enact
the stingy voting rights regime that he called for during the
Reagan years.

But if you doubt this Supreme Court's willingness to allow
one party to entrench its own rule after it gains control of a
state government, consider the Court's approach to partisan
gerrymandering.

Gerrymandering is, to be certain, a bipartisan sin. Indeed,
when the Supreme Court took up two partisan gerrymandering
cases in 2019, it picked a Republican gerrymander in North Carolina, and an equally aggressive effort to maximize Democratic
representation in Maryland. But, because redistricting typically
occurs every ten years, and because Republicans had an unusually strong performance in 2010—an election before a redistricting cycle—Republican gerrymandering shaped American
politics for a decade.

At the peak of their impact, these gerrymanders seemed to
lock a Republican majority in place in the US House of Representatives. In 2012, for example, President Obama won the state
of Ohio by about 2 percentage points, but Republicans still won
twelve of the state's sixteen House seats due to gerrymandering.
In Pennsylvania, Obama won by over 5 points, but Republicans
took home thirteen of the state's eighteen House districts. In
Michigan, Obama won by nearly 10 points, but Republicans
captured nine of the state's fourteen House seats.

50   In the years that followed, a mix of lower court decisions and demographic changes have weakened or diminished the impact of these Republican gerrymanders, but many of them remained potent years later. In 2018, for example, Wisconsin Democratic candidates won 54 percent of the votes for state assembly seats, but Republicans still won sixty-three of the assembly's niney-nine seats. Wisconsin's state legislative gerrymanders were so strong, they were virtually impervious to the will of the people.

Partisan gerrymanders also violate the First Amendment. As Justice Elena Kagan wrote in *Rucho v. Common Cause* (2019), "That Amendment gives its greatest protection to political beliefs, speech, and association." And yet, "partisan gerrymanders subject certain voters to 'disfavored treatment'—again, counting their votes for less—precisely because of 'their voting history [and] their expression of political views.'"

But Kagan's *Rucho* opinion was also a dissenting opinion. All of the Supreme Court's Republicans joined Roberts's majority opinion in that case, which held that federal courts are not even permitted to consider cases challenging partisan gerrymanders. The most aggressive partisan gerrymanders, like the ones that lock Democrats out of power in Wisconsin, remain a force today because the Supreme Court allows them to stay in place.

The Supreme Court, in other words, permitted redistricting laws that transformed legislative elections into little more than a formality in many states—because Republicans were all but certain to win no matter what the voters decided. Thanks to this Supreme Court, we already live in a world where state election laws can render the will of the people irrelevant.

And gerrymandering is likely to get much worse now that
Republicans control six seats on the Supreme Court.

States must redraw their legislative maps every ten years,
which means that every state's congressional and state legislative
maps must be updated in 2021. As a safeguard against gerrymandering, many states—including Arizona and Michigan—
plan to use independent redistricting commissions tasked with
drawing fair maps that will not give an outsized advantage to
either party. The Supreme Court upheld Arizona's redistricting
commission in *Arizona State Legislature v. Arizona Independent
Redistricting Commission* (2015).

But the Arizona case was a 5—4 decision, with retired justice
Anthony Kennedy and the late Justice Ruth Bader Ginsburg in the
majority. At least four members of the Court's current majority
appear eager to overrule *Arizona* and replace it with a rule that
could give Republican state legislatures virtually unchecked
power to draw gerrymandered maps—and a fifth member, Justice Amy Coney Barrett, has yet to weigh in on whether she is
inclined to strike down redistricting commissions.

The Constitution provides that "the Times, Places, and
Manner of holding Elections for Senators and Representatives,
shall be prescribed in each State by the Legislature thereof." For
more than a century, the Supreme Court interpreted the word
"Legislature," when used in this context, to refer to whatever the
valid lawmaking process is within a state. As Justice Ginsburg
wrote for the Court in *Arizona*, a state may determine how it will
conduct federal elections, "in accordance with the State's pre-
scriptions for lawmaking, which may include the referendum
and the Governor's veto."

Shortly before Barrett's confirmation, however, the four most conservative justices began agitating for a different reading of the word "Legislature." As Justice Gorsuch described this approach in a recent concurring opinion, "the Constitution provides that state legislatures—not federal judges, not state judges, not state governors, not other state officials—bear primary responsibility for setting election rules."

The implications of this approach are potentially breathtaking. Taken to its extreme, it means that independent redistricting commissions cannot exist (because a commission is not the state legislature). It means that the Democratic governors in states like Wisconsin, Michigan, and Pennsylvania—where Republicans control the state legislature—may not be allowed to veto legislation drawing gerrymandered congressional maps (because the governor is not part of the state legislature). And it means that state courts may not be able to enforce state constitutional provisions protecting voting rights or barring gerrymandering (because courts are not part of the state legislature either).

Republicans could gain a lock on the House of Representatives, not because they necessarily have the votes to win elections, but because the Supreme Court is likely to remove nearly all remaining safeguards against gerrymandering.

Dismantling the Administrative State

One of Justice Antonin Scalia's final acts on Earth may have been to doom the planet.

On February 9, 2016—the last Tuesday of Scalia's life—the Supreme Court handed down an unexpected order announcing that the "Environmental Protection Agency's 'Carbon Pollution Emission Guidelines for Existing Stationary Sources: Electric Utility Generating Units' is stayed." The vote was 5–4, along party lines, with Scalia joining his fellow Republicans in the majority.

The environmental regulations blocked by this order were commonly known as the Clean Power Plan, and they were the Obama administration's most ambitious effort to fight climate change. Had the Clean Power Plan taken effect, it was expected to reduce overall carbon dioxide emissions from utility power plants by 32 percent from where they were in 2005 by 2030. That's the equivalent of removing 166 million cars—or 70 percent of America's passenger vehicles—from the road entirely.

As a result, the EPA predicted that its plan would prevent "thousands of premature deaths and mean thousands fewer asthma attacks and hospitalizations in 2030 and every year beyond." And these lives would be saved at a bargain. Though EPA estimated that implementing the Clean Power Plan could cost industry as much as $8.4 billion a year in 2030, those costs would yield "public health and climate benefits worth an estimated $34 billion to $54 billion per year in 2030."

But, alas, the Clean Power Plan never took effect. Though the Supreme Court's order halting the plan was temporary, Donald Trump's 2016 victory all but ensured that the plan would not be revived. Even if the Trump administration hadn't replaced this Obama-era policy with a significantly weaker rule, the appointment of Neil Gorsuch to fill Scalia's vacant seat all but ensured that the Supreme Court would strike down the Clean Power Plan permanently if given the chance to do so.

Trump's election could prove to be one of the single most important events in human history, as it could strip the United States of its ability to address climate change for the foreseeable future. Even if President Biden wants to implement something like the Clean Power Plan, it is highly unlikely that the Supreme Court's Republican majority will let him do so.

This fight over the federal government's power to address a slow-moving catastrophe, moreover, is just one battle in a many-front war over federal agencies' power to regulate. As Steve Bannon, then the White House's chief strategist, told the Conservative Political Action Conference a month after Trump took office, one of the Trump administration's primary goals would be "deconstruction of the administrative state."

The Supreme Court is likely to permanently strip the executive branch of much of its power to issue binding regulations, and that has profound implications for nearly all areas of federal policy.

To give just a few examples, the Obama administration did not simply use its policymaking authority to create the Clean Power Plan. It also used it to bar doctors from discriminating against transgender patients. It pushed to expand overtime pay to approximately 1.3 million workers. And it required most health plans to cover a wide range of treatments, including contraceptive care.

Meanwhile, the Trump administration proposed rules weakening the ban on sexual harassment on campus, and diluting the federal ban on housing discrimination. As of November 2020, the Trump administration either rolled back, or was in the process of rolling back, 104 different regulations seeking to protect the environment.

No matter what issue you care about, in other words, it is likely that there is a federal regulation that shapes our nation's approach to that issue. And if the Supreme Court strips the government of much of its power to promulgate these regulations, it could effectively dismantle much of American law.

Finally, a quick word about Donald Trump, and the challenge his presidency lays upon liberals who have historically argued for a powerful and effective federal government. It's understandable to look at the Trump years and be grateful that the executive branch does not have more power—and to believe that strict new limits on executive power make sense to prevent men such as Trump from consolidating power.

But the Roberts Court isn't interested in such a project. This is the Court that upheld Trump's efforts to ban travelers from many predominantly Muslim nations, explaining that federal immigration law "exudes deference to the President." When lower courts blocked Trump administration policies implemented solely through executive authority—including a policy restricting transgender individuals from serving in the military, strict limits on immigrants seeking asylum, and restrictions on low-income immigrants—the Court raced to reinstate these policies.

Indeed, the Court was so solicitous toward the Trump administration that Justice Sonia Sotomayor warned that her Court was "putting a thumb on the scale" in favor of that administration.

The Supreme Court, in other words, has not shown even-handed skepticism toward executive power. It was quite permissive of President Trump's ability to aggressively wield such power, even as it is working to dismantle future presidents' ability to protect the environment, to expand access to health care, or to ensure that workers receive a fair wage.

Federal Regulation, Explained

As a general rule, Congress can regulate businesses in two different ways.

The most straightforward approach is simply to command industries to conduct their business in a certain manner. Thus, if Congress wants to reduce certain polluting emissions, it could enact a law that orders power plants to use a particular technology that reduces emissions.

But Congress is a slow-moving body, and federal laws are difficult to amend. If, in the 1970s, Congress had commanded power plants to use the best emissions reduction technology that existed at the time, it could have potentially locked these plants into using obsolete tech that is vastly inferior to the technology available now. At a minimum, Congress would have struggled to stay on top of new developments and to update this law as new methods of reducing emissions were invented.

So, when Congress wrote the Clean Air Act, it made sure that the rules governing power plants could evolve as technology improves. Under this law, power plants must update their systems for reducing emissions to ensure that they achieve the same "degree of emission limitation achievable through the application of the best system of emission reduction" that currently exists, while also accounting for factors such as cost.

Congress also gave the job of figuring out what the "best system of emission reduction" is at any particular moment to the EPA administrator. As a practical matter, that means that EPA employees who are experts on environmental regulation and the energy industry will study which new technology is available and will update the rules governing power plants as that technology evolves.

And that's exactly what EPA did when it created the Clean Power Plan. EPA determined that to achieve the "best system of emission reduction," at least some energy companies would need to shift from fairly dirty coal-fired electricity production to cleaner methods such as natural gas or renewable methods of producing energy that result in no emissions at all.

58   Rules such as this one, which are promulgated by a federal agency pursuant to a federal law permitting them to do so, are known as "regulations." When Bannon spoke of deconstructing the administrative state, a major thrust of that project involved stripping agencies of much of their ability to regulate.

Ideally, laws like the Clean Air Act make complex law-making possible without having to sacrifice democratic account-ability. Regulation allows our laws to be both democratic and dynamic. Such laws are democratic because the goals of federal policy—goals such as ensuring that power plants use the best emission-reduction technology available—are still set by the people's elected representatives in Congress. But they are dynamic because it allows federal rules to be updated without requiring Congress to enact a new law every time a new innovation is developed.

Yet, despite these advantages, the very idea that Congress should be free to delegate power in this way has many enemies within the conservative legal movement—enemies who currently wield far more power than Steve Bannon. In a 2016 opinion, for example, then judge Neil Gorsuch wrote that two foundational Supreme Court decisions preserving agencies' ability to regulate "permit executive bureaucracies to swallow huge amounts of core judicial and legislative power and concentrate federal power in a way that seems more than a little difficult to square with the Constitution of the framers' design."

After his elevation to the Supreme Court, moreover, Gorsuch called for strict new limits on the federal government's power to regulate. And five members of the Court's Republican majority have signaled, albeit in two different cases, that they agree with Gorsuch's plans to restrict agency power.

Gorsuch and his allies do not simply view Congress's power to delegate rulemaking power to agencies as undesirable. They view broad delegations of power as inconsistent with the Constitution itself. And their narrow vision of federal power has profound implications for workers, consumers, patients, and the environment. This narrow vision could also potentially leave many future presidents unable to govern.

The GOP's Shifting Position on the Administrative State

In 1989, not long after President George H. W. Bush won a landslide election and ushered in a third term of Republican rule, Justice Antonin Scalia offered a broad defense of agency regulation—and of the idea that courts should be reluctant to interfere with these agencies. "Broad delegation to the Executive is the hallmark of the modern administrative state," Scalia told an audience at Duke Law School.

Though Scalia conceded that agencies were likely to shift their regulatory approaches, depending on whether Democrats or Republicans occupied the White House, he saw these shifting approaches as a positive thing. "If Congress is to delegate broadly, as modern times are thought to demand, it seems to me desirable that the delegee be able to suit its actions to the times," Scalia said, "and that continuing political accountability be assured, through direct political pressures upon the Executive and through the indirect political pressure of congressional oversight."

Scalia offered these views just a few years after his Court handed down one of its most important decisions limiting the judiciary's power to second-guess federal agencies—*Chevron v. Natural Resources Defense Council* (1984). He would continue

60   to defend broad deference to agencies for most of his career—although he became far more critical of agency power in the Obama years.

Chevron dealt with a perennial problem that confronts all federal courts—what should be done when a federal statute is sufficiently ambiguous that it is unclear whether it permits a particular agency to promulgate a particular regulation? Under Chevron, courts generally should defer to the agency's interpretation of the law in these cases. "[I]f the statute is silent or ambiguous with respect to the specific issue" before an agency, the Court held in Chevron, "the question for the court is whether the agency's answer is based on a permissible construction of the statute."

As the Court explained, such deference to agencies is warranted for two reasons. First, agencies tend to know more about the specific policy areas they oversee, and the law governing those areas, than generalist judges. "Judges are not experts in the field," the Court explained, and they specifically lack expertise in the "competing political interests" that shape the policy-making process.

Similarly, Chevron acknowledged that regulation unavoidably requires rulemakers to make policy judgments, and it is better to leave these discretionary judgments to government officials who are accountable to an elected president, rather than placing such discretion in the hands of unelected judges. "While agencies are not directly accountable to the people, the Chief Executive is," Chevron explained. And so "it is entirely appropriate for this political branch of the Government to make such policy choices—resolving the competing interests which Congress itself either inadvertently did not resolve, or intentionally left to be resolved by the agency charged with the administration of the statute in light of everyday realities."

Chevron, in other words, was a monument to judicial humility. It recognized that the kinds of policy questions confronted by agencies—what is the "best system" for reducing emissions by power plants? Which forms of preventive care should be covered by employer health plans? Do the costs of limiting mercury emissions outweigh the benefits?—are far beyond the expertise of judges. And it recognized that, whenever possible, policy decisions should be made by elected officials or by individuals who are accountable to an elected official.

Thus, Scalia endorsed *Chevron* in 1989 because he believed that it would produce a government that was both more democratic and more dynamic than the alternative. "In the long run *Chevron* will endure," he predicted, "because it more accurately reflects the reality of government, and thus more adequately serves its needs" than a system where judges are more involved in striking down federal regulations.

Now compare Scalia's views in 1989 to the position that Gorsuch staked out in a 2016 opinion written while Gorsuch was a lower court judge. It was this case, *Gutierrez-Brizuela v. Lynch,* where Gorsuch claimed that cases like *Chevron* "permit executive bureaucracies to swallow huge amounts of core judicial and legislative power and concentrate federal power in a way that seems more than a little difficult to square with the Constitution of the framers' design." It was this case where Gorsuch labeled the federal administrative state a "behemoth" that judges must do more to confront.

62   The crux of Gorsuch's case against *Chevron* and similar cases is that it is better to give judges the final word on regulations than to give this power to federal agencies. When courts defer to agencies, Gorsuch claims, that's "a problem for the people whose liberties may now be impaired not by an independent decisionmaker seeking to declare the law's meaning as fairly as possible—the decisionmaker promised to them by law—but by an avowedly politicized administrative agent seeking to pursue whatever policy whim may rule the day."

Of course, one of *Chevron*'s core insights is that, when a federal law is truly ambiguous, someone has to resolve that ambiguity. And *Chevron* concluded that it is better to give this power to agencies that are accountable to an elected president, rather than placing that power in the hands of the closest thing the United States has to a medieval nobility—unelected judges who serve for life. Gorsuch turns this analysis on its head, presuming that judges are inherently "independent" decisionmakers who are driven solely by a desire to "declare the law's meaning as fairly as possible"—and not by the messy political concerns that might infect agencies' decisions.

But Gorsuch's insistence that judges are above politics is belied by the very job he holds today. There's a reason why Senate Republicans fought so hard to keep Obama nominee Merrick Garland off the Supreme Court, and why they fought equally hard to get someone like Gorsuch on it. Those Republicans correctly understood that Republican judges are far more likely to reach conservative outcomes than Democratic judges.

While Gorsuch himself may have a principled objection to a powerful administrative state, he owes his ability to transform that objection into national policy to the fact that the Republican

Party now believes that it benefits from a weak administrative
state. If the GOP hadn't embraced this anti-regulatory stance,
Gorsuch would almost certainly still be an obscure appeals
court judge.

A Republican White House chose Gorsuch for the Supreme
Court in large part because they expected him to take a narrow
view of federal agencies' power to regulate. As the legal journalist David Kaplan reports, "When Gorsuch became a finalist
for the Court, his opinion on Chevron deference proved deci-
sive in clinching the nomination." Though "Trump didn't read
the opinion" Gorsuch wrote slamming *Chevron*, "his advisers
did—and they told the president it was the reason to choose
Gorsuch."

So what explains the Republican Party's changing views on
administrative law? Why would a conservative icon like Scalia
praise *Chevron* in 1989, only to be replaced by an outspoken
opponent of *Chevron* a generation later?

In 1986, just a couple years after *Chevron* was decided,
federal appellate judge Kenneth Starr offered one of the most
explicit defenses of *Chevron* as a pro-democracy decision
(though Starr is widely remembered today for his role as independent counsel during the Clinton administration, in 1986
Starr was a conservative judge who would go on to become a
finalist for the Supreme Court seat that eventually went to Justice David Souter).

Judicial deference to agency regulation, Starr wrote, will
"make it easier for a new administration to carry out its electoral mandate." The fact that *Chevron* permits agencies to
"depart more easily from their predecessors' interpretations"
was a good thing, because it allowed political actors to reshape

64   regulations in the image of a popularly elected president. "In
      part because federal judges are not directly accountable to any
      electorate," Starr also claimed, "I believe they have a duty volun-
      tarily to exercise 'judicial restraint.'"

      But who was likely to control the "new administration"
      that Starr wrote about when he praised *Chevron*? In mid-1986,
      around the time Starr wrote his article praising *Chevron*, Pres-
      ident Reagan had an astounding 68 percent approval rating.
      Reagan dominated both of his presidential races, and his vice
      president would go on to trounce Democratic nominee Michael
      Dukakis in 1988. Republicans correctly believed that they had a
      strong popular mandate in the 1980s.

      At the same time, the courts were far less conservative in
      the 1980s than they are today, with many judgeships still held
      by liberal Kennedy, Johnson, or Carter appointees who might
      interfere with Reagan's deregulatory plans if given a broad
      power to do so.

      Republicans, in other words, had every reason to prefer
      presidential power to judicial power in the 1980s, because they
      had a much more secure grasp on the executive branch than they
      did on the judiciary. Decisions like *Chevron* required judges to
      get out of Reagan and Bush's way.

      Modern-day Republicans, by contrast, face the oppo-
      site dilemma. Republicans like Gorsuch absolutely domi-
      nate the federal bench, and Republicans have a solid majority
      on the Supreme Court. Yet, as President Biden's recent elec-
      tion shows, the GOP has a much weaker grasp on executive
      power. There's a reason why conservative opposition to agency
      rulemaking crescendoed during the Obama years. And, even

though a Republican succeeded President Obama, Trump did so only after losing the popular vote by nearly three million ballots.

By shifting power from federal agencies to the judiciary, in other words, Republicans also shift authority to their most secure base of power.

The GOP is unlikely to lose its grip on the judiciary any time soon. Because the Senate gives tiny red states like Wyoming exactly the same number of senators as large blue states like California—despite the fact that California has nearly sixty-eight times as many people as Wyoming—means that Democrats need an commanding majority to have any shot of controlling the Senate.

In the current Senate, Democratic senators represent more than forty million more people than Republicans. And yet the Senate is evenly divided between the two parties.

That means that Republicans are hugely favored to hold the Senate in future elections, regardless of whether the voters prefer Democratic control. And GOP control of the Senate will give Republicans the power to block any Democratic judicial nominations and the power to block legislation writing federal regulations into a statute.

Selective Deference
There are troubling signs that, contrary to Gorsuch's suggestion that judges are apolitical actors who "declare the law's meaning as fairly as possible," many of the Court's Republicans would replace the broad deference judges owed agencies under cases like *Chevron* with more selective deference. Judges like Gorsuch and Kavanaugh appear to be very troubled by agency

power—except when that power is used to skew political power toward Republicans.

Consider a pair of administrative law cases—one obscure, the other very high-profile—that the Court decided on subsequent days in June of 2019. The first of these two cases is *Kisor v. Wilkie* (2019), and it features one of Gorsuch's most full-throated attacks on the idea that agency officials can be trusted to shape policy.

Kisor involved a doctrine, known as "Auer deference" after the Supreme Court's decision in *Auer v. Robbins* (1997), which requires courts to defer to "agencies' reasonable readings of genuinely ambiguous regulations." That is, just as *Chevron* calls for courts to defer to an agency's reading of an ambiguous statute, *Auer* instructs courts to apply similar deference when an agency's own regulation contains ambiguous language.

The outcome in *Kisor* was messy, with the four most conservative justices arguing that *Auer* should be abandoned entirely, and a majority of the Court agreeing to retain *Auer*—while also warning that courts should be hesitant to apply *Auer* deference too broadly. For the purposes of this book, the most significant aspect of *Kisor* are several lines in Gorsuch's separate opinion, which suggest that judicial deference to agency judgments is something akin to tyranny.

If agencies can shape federal policy, Gorsuch warned, ordinary Americans "are left always a little unsure what the law is, at the mercy of political actors and the shifting winds of popular opinion, and without the chance for a fair hearing before a neutral judge." In such a world, he claims, "the rule of law begins to bleed into the rule of men."

Indeed, much of Gorsuch's opinion suggests that judges are inherently more trustworthy than employees of the executive branch, and that judges should accordingly be given far more power. "Unlike Article III judges," Gorsuch claims, "executive officials are not, nor are they supposed to be, 'wholly impartial.'" If the courts permit executive branch officials to act, Gorsuch continues, those officials are likely to push "their own interests, their own constituencies, and their own policy goals—and when interpreting a regulation, they may choose to 'press the case for the side [they] represen[t].'"

Bear this criticism of executive branch officials in mind as you consider a case the Supreme Court handed down just one day after *Kisor*.

The Court's decision in *Department of Commerce v. New York* (2019) received far more public attention than the more technical question presented in *Kisor. New York* involved the Trump administration's effort to add a question to the 2020 census's main form asking respondents if they are United States citizens. Census experts from both parties, and from within the Census Bureau itself, all warned the administration not to include such a question because it would discourage many immigrants from responding to the census, and because it would lead to inaccurate data.

The Fourteenth Amendment provides that "representatives shall be apportioned among the several states according to their respective numbers, counting the whole number of persons in each state." So all residents of the United States must be counted, regardless of whether they are citizens, and regardless of their immigration status. But the Census Bureau's own

68   experts predicted that including a citizenship question on the 2020 census form would lead to a "5.1 percent decline in response rates among noncitizen households."

As top census officials from the Reagan and first Bush administration explained to Congress, a citizenship question "could seriously jeopardize the accuracy of the census," because "people who are undocumented immigrants may either avoid the census altogether or deliberately misreport themselves as legal residents." Legal residents, meanwhile, "may misunderstand or mistrust the census and fail or refuse to respond."

So why include such a question at all? The most likely answer to this question came from the late Republican strategist Thomas Hofeller, a leading GOP expert on gerrymandering, who urged the Trump administration to include the citizenship question on census forms. In leaked documents, revealed while the *New York* case was still pending before the Supreme Court, Hofeller argued that a citizenship question would "clearly be a disadvantage to the Democrats" and "advantageous to Republicans and Non-Hispanic Whites."

The Trump administration never publicly admitted that this partisan objective was a reason to include a citizenship question on the census form. Instead, Commerce Secretary Wilbur Ross claimed that he planned to add the citizenship question "at the request of the Department of Justice (DOJ), which sought improved data about citizen voting-age population for purposes of enforcing the Voting Rights Act."

This explanation was implausible on its face. For one thing, Trump's Justice Department didn't show much interest in Voting Rights Act enforcement. The census, moreover, hasn't asked a citizenship question on its main form since 1950, and the Voting Rights Act didn't become law until 1965. So Voting Rights Act enforcement has never depended on the kind of data the Trump administration claimed to have sought.

Moreover, as the Supreme Court explained in *New York*, there is considerable evidence suggesting that the administration invented this Voting Rights Act–based justification after it had already decided to move forward with the citizenship question:

> That evidence showed that the Secretary was determined to reinstate a citizenship question from the time he entered office; instructed his staff to make it happen; waited while Commerce officials explored whether another agency would request census-based citizenship data; subsequently contacted the Attorney General himself to ask if DOJ would make the request; and adopted the Voting Rights Act rationale late in the process. In the District Court's view, this evidence established that the Secretary had made up his mind to reinstate a citizenship question "well before" receiving DOJ's request, and did so for reasons unknown but unrelated to the VRA.

All of this evidence was enough to convince Chief Justice Roberts that, at the very least, the government cannot lie to the public and the judiciary when it justifies its own decisions. The Trump administration's explanation for why it included a citizenship question, Roberts wrote for himself and his four liberal colleagues, "rested on a pretextual basis," and that was enough reason to remove the citizenship question from the 2020 form. (*New York* was decided before Justice Ruth Bader Ginsburg's death, when Roberts and the liberal justices still added up to a majority.)

This fairly basic conclusion—that the government may not tell outright lies about why it adopted a policy that was likely to shift power from Democrats and toward Republicans—garnered a livid response from the Court's most conservative members.

The primary dissent in *New York* was authored by Justice Clarence Thomas, and joined by both Gorsuch and Kavanaugh. It begins by railing against the idea that courts should question the motives of agency officials. "The Court's holding reflects an unprecedented departure from our deferential review of discretionary agency decisions," Thomas wrote. He continues that the problem with the majority opinion is that it is easy for an administration's political opponents to cast doubt upon an agency's actions, and courts shouldn't be swayed by those efforts.

"It is not difficult for political opponents of executive actions to generate controversy with accusations of pretext, deceit, and illicit motives," according to Thomas. And if judges are allowed to dig into those accusations, agency actions could be tied up in an "endless morass of discovery and policy disputes." Worse, Thomas goes on to question the motives of *judges* who would second-guess the agency's decision regarding the census question—likening an implication that the Trump administration lied about its motives to a baseless conspiracy theory.

"I do not deny," Thomas says, "that a judge predisposed to distrust the Secretary or the administration could arrange those facts on a corkboard and—with a jar of pins and a spool of string—create an eye-catching conspiracy web," which would suggest that maybe the Trump administration didn't have the most pure motives for including a census question that hasn't been used since the Jim Crow Era, and that was likely to shift power to Republican communities.

Thomas, in other words, calls for extraordinary deference to agency officials accused of lying—to the point of likening some of his own colleagues to conspiracy-obsessed madmen because they questioned the Trump administration's motives. But this is the very same Justice Thomas who, one day earlier, joined Gorsuch's opinion in *Kisor*.

That opinion, you may recall, warned that agency officials are inherently untrustworthy because they "are not, nor are they supposed to be, 'wholly impartial.'" It dismissed executive branch officials as consumed by "their own interests, their own constituencies, and their own policy goals," and warned that they are prone "to 'press the case for the side [they] represen[t].'" And it suggested that the only cure for this inherent partisanship is "a fair hearing before a neutral judge."

So which one is it? Are executive branch officials inherent partisans who cannot be trusted without judicial supervision, as Gorsuch suggested in *Kisor*, or are they public servants who must be shielded from judicial inquiry into their motives, as Thomas suggested in *New York*? Read together, the most conservative justices' opinions in *Kisor* and *New York* are hard to square with one another.

It is, frankly, difficult to read the dissenting opinions in *New York* without coming to deeply unsettling conclusions about the justices who joined those opinions. Here we see judges who have largely maintained a principled (if highly disruptive) position of distrust toward federal agencies, suddenly deciding that an agency is owed extraordinary deference. And we see them

72   doing so in a case that could have shifted political power from
Democrats to Republicans.

At the very least, the most conservative justices' position
in *New York* is inconsistent with the approach they take in other
administrative law cases. At worst, the *New York* dissents suggest that these justices are willing to put partisan gain ahead of
their legal principles.

The Future of Judicial Review of Agency Actions

Chevron, Auer, Kisor, and *New York* are all important decisions,
but they all involve relatively marginal questions in administrative law—questions like whether Congress has delegated a
particular power to an agency, or whether an agency uses its delegated power appropriately. But the Roberts Court's most significant attack on the administrative state involves a much more
fundamental question: whether Congress is allowed to delegate
regulatory power to agencies in the first place.

At least five of the Supreme Court's Republicans support
reviving the "nondelegation doctrine," the largely defunct idea
that the Constitution places strict limits on Congress's ability
to delegate power to federal agencies—although these five justices have yet to declare nondelegation the law of the land in a
majority opinion.

The nondelegation doctrine rests on the thinnest of constitutional reeds. The Constitution gives Congress the "legislative" power and the president and the various federal agencies
that answer to the president the "executive" power. The legislative power, according to Gorsuch, is the power to "adopt generally applicable rules of conduct governing future actions by

private persons." And the Constitution must place strict limits
on Congress's ability to delegate this power to agencies merely
tasked with executing existing laws.

Often, proponents of the nondelegation doctrine quote a
passage from the political philosopher John Locke—claiming
that "the legislative cannot transfer the power of making laws
to any other hands; for it being but a delegated power from the
people, they who have it cannot pass it over to others"—to support their argument that Congress may not delegate the power
to make binding rules to the executive branch.

But there are many problems with this account of Congress's ability to delegate power. For one thing, it misunder-
stands Locke. As law professors Julian Davis Mortenson and
Nicholas Bagley note in an important paper, Locke draws a distinction between the legislature's ability to "transfer" power,
and a "delegated" power. Transferring a power requires a "permanent alienation"—that is, for Congress to "transfer" legislative power, it would have to give up that power forever to some
other person or body. But Locke raised no objection to a legislature delegating a power, meaning that lawmakers may assign the
ability to make certain binding rules to an agency, so long as the
legislature retains the ability to take that power back.

Indeed, if anything, Locke's quote undercuts the argument
for the nondelegation doctrine because it recognizes that the
legislative power has already been delegated once—to the legislature itself. Locke describes the power to make laws as "a
delegated power from the people." That is, it is the people, not
the Congress or some other representative body, that has the
inherent power to make rules that bind the whole of society.

74   When the Constitution created Congress, it delegated the people's power to make laws to that Congress. And Congress may, in
turn, delegate a portion of that power to federal agencies.

Congress's early history supports this reading of the Constitution, as the very first Congress enacted numerous laws
giving vast discretion to other government officials. It allowed
officials overseeing the Northwest Territory to "adopt and pub-
lish in the district, such laws of the original States, criminal and
civil, as may be necessary, and best suited to the circumstances
of the district." It delegated Congress's entire power to provide
patents to inventors to executive branch officials, allowing the
secretary of state, the secretary of war, or the attorney general to
grant patents so long as they "deem the invention or discovery
sufficiently useful or important."

The First Congress didn't simply give executive branch
officials the power to issue licenses that would allow merchants to trade with Native American tribes; it also allowed the
executive to promulgate regulations that would govern license
holders "in all things touching the said trade and intercourse."
The First Congress allowed the president to identify wounded
or disabled soldiers, and to place them on "the list of the inva-
lids of the United States, at such rate of pay, and under such
regulations, as shall be directed by the President of the United
States, for the time being." And it delegated to "any common
law court of record" the power to grant citizenship to any free
white person who resided in the country for two years, provided
that the court was satisfied that the new citizen is a "person of
good character."

Long-standing Supreme Court precedents, moreover, are
consistent with the framers' view that Congress has a broad

authority to delegate power, so long as it does not do so irre-
vocably. As the Court explained in *Mistretta v. United States*
(1989), "In our increasingly complex society, replete with
ever changing and more technical problems, Congress simply
cannot do its job absent an ability to delegate power under
broad general directives." Thus, the Court has explained, Congress may delegate regulatory power to agencies so long as it
"shall lay down by legislative act an intelligible principle to
which the person or body authorized to [exercise the delegated
authority] is directed to conform."

And yet, the Court now appears likely to abandon this long-
standing rule.

In early October of 2018, just a few days before Justice Kavanaugh was confirmed to the Supreme Court, the eight remaining
justices heard *Gundy v. United States* (2019), a case brought by a
convicted sex offender who challenged his conviction for failing
to register as a sex offender when he moved to New York. Specifically, Herman Gundy challenged a federal statute that allowed
the Justice Department to determine which sex offenders, who
were convicted before a certain date, had to register with their
state governments (the Justice Department determined that *all*
eligible offenders must register).

Gundy's lawyers argued that Congress did not lawfully delegate the power to decide which sex offenders must register to a
federal agency.

Gorsuch used his opinion in *Gundy* to criticize the long-
standing rule laid out in cases like *Mistretta*. Warning that permitting Congress to delegate power to agencies risks giving
those agencies "unbounded policy choices," Gorsuch proposed
a vague new limit on Congress's power to delegate. According to

76   Gorsuch, delegations of power to agencies must be struck down unless Congress sets "forth standards 'sufficiently definite and precise to enable Congress, the courts, and the public to ascertain' whether Congress's guidance has been followed."

This vague new standard is inconsistent with the First Congress's understanding of the Constitution. And it would effectively consolidate an enormous amount of power within the judiciary.

As a practical matter, when the Supreme Court hands down a vague and open-ended legal standard like the one Gorsuch articulated in his *Gundy* opinion, the Court is shifting power to itself. What does it mean for a statute to be "sufficiently definite and precise" that the public can "ascertain whether Congress's guidance has been followed"? The answer is that the courts—and, ultimately, the Supreme Court—will decide for themselves what this vague language means. The courts will gain a broad new power to strike down federal regulations, on the grounds that they exceed Congress's power to delegate authority.

In theory, that could mean that federal regulations will simply receive more scrutiny from an impartial judiciary—the "fair hearing before a neutral judge" that Gorsuch spoke of in *Kisor*. But, in practice, the judiciary is only as good as the judges who staff it. The same four justices who dissented in *New York* will have a significant voice in which regulations are upheld and which regulations are struck down—and they will only need to convince either the conservative chief justice or Justice Barrett if they want to repeal a particular regulation.

Indeed, the Court has already signaled that it intends to use the nondelegation doctrine to roll back access to health care.

In *Little Sisters v. Pennsylvania* (2020), the Supreme Court considered a provision of the Affordable Care Act allowing a federal agency to determine which forms of "preventive care and screenings" for women must be covered without copays or other out-of-pocket costs by health insurers. Among other things, the agency determined that contraceptive care must be covered.

Yet Justice Thomas's majority opinion strongly suggests that this provision of the Affordable Care Act violates the nondelegation doctrine: He accuses Congress of giving "virtually unbridled discretion to decide what counts as preventive care and screenings" to a federal agency. It is likely, in other words, that the Supreme Court will soon strike down the requirement that health insurers cover birth control—and it may strike down other, similarly worded provisions of Obamacare requiring coverage of immunizations and pediatric care.

The Court's majority, in other words, already appears to have big plans for how it will start remaking American law under this nondelegation doctrine.

It should be noted that Gorsuch's opinion in *Gundy* was technically a dissent—the opinion was joined only by Roberts and Justice Thomas—but Justices Alito and Kavanaugh have both signaled in other opinions that they share Gorsuch's desire to revive the nondelegation doctrine. And *Little Sisters* leaves little doubt that a majority of the Court is eager to reinstate this doctrine. Thus, it is most likely only a matter of time before the Court takes up Gorsuch's charge to consolidate its own power over federal regulation.

In the likely event that Gorsuch's views do prevail, that would be a sea change in American administrative law. The common thread uniting decisions such as *Chevron, Auer,* and *Mistretta* is deference to elected branches. Courts should defer to Congress's decision that the best way to achieve a particular policy objective is to delegate regulatory power to a federal agency. And they should defer to agencies when the law or a regulation is uncertain.

As the Court recognized in *Chevron,* judges "are not part of either political branch." They have no democratic legitimacy. And so, it is more appropriate to allow lawmakers or an executive branch that is accountable to the voters to make "policy choices" than to place that power in the hands of unelected judges.

There is, of course, a real risk that either Congress or the executive will use its power unwisely. There is even a risk that these bodies will abuse their power. But the alternative to judicial deference is worse. It means placing unchecked power in the hands of men and women who serve for life, and who may be no less partisan than the people who can be voted out of office if they use their power irresponsibly.

Religion

Maurice Bessinger was a racist.

Locally famous for Maurice's Piggie Park, a South Carolina restaurant chain that sells smoked pork doused in the yellow, mustard-based sauce particular to the state, Bessinger built a multimillion-dollar barbecue empire that once sold its frozen barbecue well beyond South Carolina. At the peak of his business, Bessinger's barbecue was sold at Walmart, and provided to servicemembers by the United States military—though he lost those customers after they learned about Bessinger's peculiar ideology.

For many years, Bessinger sold white supremacist tracts at his restaurants, even offering a discount on food to customers who bought the racist literature. One of these screeds proclaimed that African slaves "blessed the Lord for allowing them to be enslaved and sent to America." After Congress prohibited restaurants from engaging in racial discrimination in 1964, Bessinger reportedly posted an uncensored version of a sign

80   proclaiming that "[t]he law makes us serve n***ers, but any money we get from them goes to the Ku Klux Klan."

Nor did Bessinger simply sell racist literature and post menacing signs to drive African Americans away from his business. He also claimed to have Jesus on his side.

The Civil Rights Act of 1964's ban on whites-only lunch counters, Bessinger claimed in a federal lawsuit, "contravenes the will of God," and cannot be applied to Bessinger's restaurants because it "constitutes an interference with the 'free exercise of [his] religion.'"

But the Supreme Court that heard *Newman v. Piggie Park Enterprises* (1968) could not have been more dismissive of Bessinger's claim that his faith gives him a right to discriminate. In a footnote to an unsigned opinion, the justices declared that *Piggie Park* "is not even a borderline case." Indeed, Bessinger's claim that his religion licenses hate was "so patently frivolous" that it would be "manifestly inequitable" to require the plaintiffs to pay for their own attorney—Bessinger would have to cover the costs of suing him into compliance with the law.

The notion that religion could be used to immunize a business owner from an anti-discrimination law, the Supreme Court understood in 1968, was so ridiculous that it warranted little discussion beyond a disdainful footnote.

Nor was this understanding that religion does not provide a right to discriminate limited to race discrimination cases. Fremont Christian School is a private school in California that, at least in the 1980s, offered a very unusual benefits package to its employees. The school's faith taught that "in any marriage, the husband is the head of the household and is required to provide for that household." Accordingly, the school typically did not offer health insurance to its married women employees, because it believed that it was that woman's husband's job to provide her with such benefits. Male employees and unmarried women, by contrast, were provided with a health plan.

The Fremont Christian case never reached the Supreme Court, but a federal appeals court that dealt with the school's claim that its religion permitted it to engage in sex discrimination took that claim little more seriously than Maurice Bessinger's arguments in *Piggie Park*. Congress's goal of banning sex discrimination, the court explained, is "equally if not more compelling than other interests that have been held to justify legislation that burdened the exercise of religious convictions."

The right to freely practice one's faith—or, in the First Amendment's words, the right to "free exercise" of religion—is a foundational freedom. But, until very recently, this freedom was never understood to allow one person to wield their faith to cut away the rights of another. And the right to Free Exercise certainly did not permit businesses to ignore laws that bind their competitors.

Again, as the Supreme Court held in *United States v. Lee* (1982), "When followers of a particular sect enter into commercial activity as a matter of choice, the limits they accept on their own conduct as a matter of conscience and faith are not to be superimposed on the statutory schemes which are binding on others in that activity."

But this long-standing view, that the rights of the faithful do not trump the rights of nonbelievers, is under heavy fire from the Roberts Court. Indeed, it is very likely that the Court's Republican majority will hold that business owners have a constitutional right to defy at least some anti-discrimination

82 laws—just so long as those owners claim a religious justification for their decision to discriminate.

For many years, the Court's religion cases focused on relatively marginal issues—such as whether states can erect explicitly religious monuments or under what circumstances states
may fund religious education. These issues remain live in the
current Court—indeed, the Roberts Court has moved the law
significantly to the right on both of these issues.

But the question of whether people of faith may seek
exemptions from the law, even when such exemptions undercut
the rights of others, has far more sweeping implications. It
could allow the Court to insulate religious conservatives from
much of the law, permitting them to ignore obligations that are
binding on all other Americans.

A Brief History of Religious Exemptions
to Federal and State Laws

One of the toughest challenges facing judges hearing religious
liberty lawsuits is balancing the rights of the faithful with the
basic rule that everyone in a society should be bound by the
same laws. On the one hand, the Constitution's ban on laws
"prohibiting the free exercise" of religion indicates that there
are some aspects of people's spiritual lives that the government
simply cannot touch. On the other hand, as Maurice Bessinger's attempt to use religion to shield racism demonstrates, faith
cannot grant a license to ignore any law that the person of faith
objects to on religious grounds.

If any person can exempt themselves from any law that cuts
against their religious belief, the Supreme Court warned nearly
a century and a half ago, then such a system risks making "the

professed doctrines of religious belief superior to the law of the land, and in effect to permit every citizen to become a law unto himself."

The modern cases governing what happens when a religious objector seeks an exemption from a state or federal law begin with *Sherbert v. Verner* (1963), a case involving a Seventh-day Adventist who refused to work on Saturday because that day is honored as the sabbath in her faith.

The plaintiff in *Sherbert* sought unemployment benefits from the state of South Carolina after she lost her job, but South Carolina denied such benefits to anyone who "has failed, without good cause ... to accept available suitable work," and this plaintiff refused to take any job that required her to work on Saturday. The question was whether the Free Exercise Clause permitted South Carolina to deny unemployment benefits to someone who would otherwise be eligible for them, except for the fact that they refused to act against their own religious beliefs.

The Court ruled in favor of this plaintiff, and some of the language in *Sherbert* suggests that the Constitution gives absolutely sweeping protections to religious objectors. South Carolina's restrictions on Saturday Sabbatarians, the Court held, must advance "some compelling state interest" in order to be permissible under the Constitution.

This "compelling state interest" language will be familiar to any law student who has completed their first semester of constitutional law. When the government engages in activity that is particularly odious to the Constitution—activity such as race discrimination or direct censorship of political viewpoints—courts will strike down that activity unless the government's

84   actions are "precisely tailored to serve a compelling governmental interest." This test, known as "strict scrutiny," is one of
the toughest tests the Court can impose in a constitutional case.
Most laws subjected to strict scrutiny are struck down.

Yet *Sherbert* also contains some language indicating that
courts should be more cautious about granting legal exemptions to religious objectors than its use of the words "compelling state interest" suggests. For one thing, *Sherbert* strongly
implies that someone with a religious objection to a particular
law may not use that objection to "abridge any other person's
religious liberties." *Sherbert* also indicates that a business owner
should not be afforded a religious exemption to a particular law
if such an exemption would give that business owner too great
of a "competitive advantage" over their competitors.

Thus, for example, a business may not claim that its owner
objects to paying the minimum wage on religious grounds, and
thus gain a competitive advantage over other businesses who
must comply with such a law.

Courts applying *Sherbert* to future cases often claimed that
they were applying the same strict scrutiny test to religious
objectors that they also applied to laws that discriminated on
the basis of race. But the data does not bear this claim out. In
1992, James E. Ryan, a legal scholar who now serves as president
of the University of Virginia, examined all ninety-seven Free
Exercise cases applying the "compelling interest" test that federal appeals courts heard between 1980 and 1990. Those courts
rejected eighty-five of these ninety-seven claims.

Another study by UCLA law professor Adam Winkler indicates that a similar pattern continued into the next decade.

According to Winkler, between 1990 and 2003, federal courts applying the compelling interest test upheld only 22 percent of free speech restrictions and 27 percent of laws engaged in racial or similar discrimination—but these courts upheld 59 percent of "religious liberty burdens." Courts, in other words, were much more likely to uphold burdens on religious practice than they were to uphold race discrimination, government censorship, or other kinds of laws that are subject to strict scrutiny.

The fact that courts continued to rule against most religious objectors throughout the 1990s and even into the 2000s is significant, moreover, because the law governing religious liberty suits changed dramatically in this period.

In 1990, the Supreme Court decided *Employment Division v. Smith*, a case involving members of a Native American faith who wished to use the hallucinogenic drug peyote in one of their sacred rituals. The question in the case is whether these two men, like the plaintiff in *Sherbert*, had a constitutional right to practice one of their religious traditions, even when that tradition violated a criminal ban on the use of peyote.

Justice Antonin Scalia's majority opinion in *Smith* carved out a massive exemption to *Sherbert*'s compelling interest test. "The right of free exercise," Scalia wrote, "does not relieve an individual of the obligation to comply with a 'valid and neutral law of general applicability,'" simply because that individual objects to that law on religious grounds.

Scalia's reasons for this holding were largely practical. And they hearken back to the Court's warning from more than a century ago that too-expansive protections for religious objectors are an invitation to anarchy:

The government's ability to enforce generally applicable prohibitions of socially harmful conduct, like its ability to carry out other aspects of public policy, "cannot depend on measuring the effects of a governmental action on a religious objector's spiritual development." To make an individual's obligation to obey such a law contingent upon the law's coincidence with his religious beliefs, except where the State's interest is "compelling"—permitting him, by virtue of his beliefs, "to become a law unto himself"—contradicts both constitutional tradition and common sense.

Smith, however, was not a beloved opinion. And it almost immediately triggered a bipartisan backlash. Led by Senators Ted Kennedy (D-MA) and Orrin Hatch (R-UT) in the Senate, and then representative Chuck Schumer (D-NY) in the House, Congress voted overwhelmingly to enact the Religious Freedom Restoration Act of 1993 (RFRA)—which sought to overrule *Smith*. The RFRA statute's explicit purpose is to "restore the compelling interest test as set forth in *Sherbert v. Verner*" and in another, closely related, case.

Under RFRA, the government "may substantially burden a person's exercise of religion only if it demonstrates that application of the burden to the person . . . is in furtherance of a compelling governmental interest" and that the government used "the least restrictive means of furthering that compelling governmental interest." Substantial burdens on religion, in other words, must survive strict scrutiny.

A likely explanation for why RFRA enjoyed such broad support among Democrats, at least at the time of its enactment, is that *Smith* was widely viewed as a blow to minority faiths—such as the Native American worshipers who wished to use sacramental peyote—when it was handed down. As Justice Sandra Day O'Connor wrote in an opinion disagreeing with Scalia's approach to the First Amendment's Free Exercise Clause, "the First Amendment was enacted precisely to protect the rights of those whose religious practices are not shared by the majority and may be viewed with hostility."

Lawmakers are much less likely to enact laws that burden faiths that are widely represented in the electorate because many members of those faiths are likely to serve in the legislature, and to oppose such burdens. But minority sects are less likely to be able to defend themselves in the political process, and thus require special protection from the courts.

Many of the law's Democratic supporters were quite explicit that they viewed RFRA as an uncontroversial statute that, in Senator Kennedy's words, would operate "only to overturn the Supreme Court's decision in Smith," without "unsettl[ing] other areas of the law." As Justice Ruth Bader Ginsburg later wrote, "Congress expected courts considering RFRA claims to 'look to free exercise cases decided prior to Smith for guidance.'"

That meant that cases like *Lee*, with its holding that business owners may not impose "the limits they accept on their own conduct as a matter of conscience and faith" upon others, remained binding under RFRA. It also meant that Ryan and Winkler's finding that courts apply strict scrutiny less rigorously to religious objectors than they apply it in other contexts should continue to hold in a post-RFRA world.

But as the Court grew more conservative, it started to read RFRA far more expansively.

88   Hobby Lobby Abandons Decades of Prior Law

Burwell v. Hobby Lobby is a perfect encapsulation of the Obama-era culture wars. It involved the Affordable Care Act, the law most hated by Republicans of this era. And it involved questions of religion, sexuality, and even abortion.

The Affordable Care Act requires most employee health plans to provide "'preventive care and screenings' for women without 'any cost sharing requirements.'" An Obama-era regulation, moreover, defines "preventive care and screenings" to include all forms of contraception approved by the Food and Drug Administration. Thus, nearly all employers were required to include birth control coverage in their employees' health plans. (It's worth noting that providing such coverage typically costs employers nothing, because covering the cost of contraception is cheaper than covering the cost of pregnancy.)

The plaintiffs in *Hobby Lobby* were business owners who (falsely) believed that four forms of birth control—two forms of emergency contraception and two kinds of intrauterine devices—are abortifacients and thus conflict with their religious objections to abortion. They sued under RFRA, claiming a right to exclude these four forms of contraception from their employees' health plans.

If the Supreme Court had applied the same law that existed prior to *Smith*—the law that much of Congress thought it endorsed when it enacted RFRA—then *Hobby Lobby* would have been an open-and-shut case. *Lee* held, again, that "[w]hen followers of a particular sect enter into commercial activity as a matter of choice, the limits they accept on their own conduct as a matter of conscience and faith are not to be superimposed on the statutory schemes which are binding on others in that activity." And the *Hobby Lobby* plaintiffs were all followers of a particular sect who entered into commercial activity as a matter of choice.

But Justice Samuel Alito's majority opinion in *Hobby Lobby* got around this problem by divorcing RFRA from the Court's previous First Amendment decisions.

Recall that RFRA limits the government's ability to "substantially burden a person's exercise of religion." As originally drafted, RFRA defined the term "exercise of religion" as "the exercise of religion under the First Amendment." In 2000, however, Congress amended this definition to state that the "exercise of religion" includes "any exercise of religion, whether or not compelled by, or central to, a system of religious belief." According to Alito, this amendment was "an obvious effort to effect a complete separation from First Amendment case law." Courts applying RFRA, according to Alito, were no longer bound by pre-RFRA decisions like *Lee.*

But there's nothing "obvious" about Alito's reading of this 2000 amendment. Among other things, the amended RFRA statute still states that the purpose of RFRA is "to restore the compelling interest test as set forth in *Sherbert v. Verner* and *Wisconsin v. Yoder*," two pre-RFRA First Amendment decisions. So the RFRA statute itself states fairly clearly that at least some of the Court's "First Amendment case law" should remain applicable to RFRA suits.

The upshot of Alito's opinion is that courts hearing cases brought by religious objectors will no longer apply the modest version of strict scrutiny chronicled in Ryan and Winkler's

90   research. Rather, courts must now apply the "exceptionally demanding" version of strict scrutiny that they typically apply to laws that discriminate on the basis of race or that engage in government censorship.

It should be noted that there is one important limit on this holding. In *City of Boerne v. Flores* (1997), the Court held that RFRA does not apply to state laws that burden religious practice. Only the federal government must comply with RFRA's demands—although, as we will see, it is likely that the Court will soon extend *Hobby Lobby*'s expansive definition of "religious liberty" to state laws as well.

Nevertheless, the implications of *Hobby Lobby* stretch far beyond Obamacare's birth control regulations. Among other things, as Justice Ginsburg warned in her dissenting opinion, *Hobby Lobby* creates a real risk that the Supreme Court may grant exemptions to people with religious objections to anti-discrimination laws.

And it now seems likely that Ginsburg's fears will become a reality.

The Future of Religious Exceptions to the Law

Masterpiece Cakeshop v. Colorado Civil Rights Commission (2018) was the Roberts Court's first foray into the question of whether religious objectors may claim a right to violate anti-discrimination law. And, while *Masterpiece* ended somewhat inconclusively, it most likely portends a significant new expansion of the rights of such objectors.

The case involved Jack Phillips, a baker who refused to make a wedding cake for a gay couple because doing so would offend Phillips's religious objection to same-sex marriage. Among

other things, the baker claimed that requiring him to obey a
Colorado law forbidding discrimination on the basis of sexual
orientation violated his right to freely exercise his religious
beliefs.

Justice Anthony Kennedy's majority opinion in *Masterpiece*—one of the last opinions Kennedy wrote before his retire-
ment—largely avoids the big questions presented by this case.
Instead, Kennedy gave Phillips a very narrow victory, arguing
that the Colorado state agency charged with enforcing many of
the state's civil rights laws showed "some elements of a clear
and impermissible hostility toward the sincere religious beliefs
that motivated [the baker's] objection."

Specifically, Kennedy appeared particularly offended by
a comment from one of the state's civil rights commissioners,
which warned against the consequences of allowing religion to
justify wrongful acts:

> I would also like to reiterate what we said in the hearing or the
> last meeting. Freedom of religion and religion has been used
> to justify all kinds of discrimination throughout history,
> whether it be slavery, whether it be the holocaust, whether
> it be—I mean, we—we can list hundreds of situations where
> freedom of religion has been used to justify discrimination.
> And to me it is one of the most despicable pieces of rhetoric
> that people can use to—to use their religion to hurt others.

Religion has indeed been used throughout history to justify discrimination. It was used to defend slavery—indeed,
some early American theologians argued that slavery was an
act of providence because it allowed enslaved people to become

Christians and thus save their souls. The Supreme Court itself has called out state officials for using religion to justify discrimination. In *Loving v. Virginia* (1967), the seminal decision striking down racial marriage discrimination, the Court rejected the reasoning of a state trial judge who argued that bans on interracial marriage are justified because "Almighty God created the races white, black, yellow, malay and red, and he placed them on separate continents," and "the fact that he separated the races shows that he did not intend for the races to mix."

Nevertheless, Kennedy deemed the Colorado civil rights commissioner's statement to be beyond the pale. "To describe a man's faith as 'one of the most despicable pieces of rhetoric that people can use' is to disparage his religion in at least two distinct ways," Kennedy wrote. To Kennedy, such a statement disparages Phillips's religious beliefs "by describing it as despicable, and also by characterizing it as merely rhetorical—something insubstantial and even insincere."

The upshot of this decision is that Colorado may still enforce its civil rights laws—indeed, Kennedy also wrote that "it is unexceptional that Colorado law can protect gay persons" from discrimination—but state officials tasked with doing so must be scrupulously polite to people who raise religious objections to civil rights laws. A stray remark can potentially undermine the state's case against someone like Jack Phillips.

Kennedy, however, is no longer on the Court. And his unsatisfying answer to what should happen when an individual claims a religious right to discriminate is unlikely to be the last word on this question. Much of the action in *Masterpiece Cakeshop* took place outside of Kennedy's majority opinion, where

Justices Elena Kagan and Neil Gorsuch battled over the very nature of religious liberty claims.

One side issue that arose in *Masterpiece* is what should happen to a baker with the opposite views as Phillips. Suppose, for example, that a baker with pro-equality views is asked to bake a cake with an anti-gay message. May this baker refuse to bake such a cake? And, if so, why is the government allowed to discriminate in favor of people with pro-gay religious views, and against people like Phillips?

Justice Kagan offered a simple way out of this conundrum. A merchant may refuse to sell a particular product altogether. A baker may simply tell their anti-gay customer that he will not bake a cake that displays an anti-gay message for anyone— regardless of their sexual orientation. Phillips, similarly, could refuse to bake wedding cakes altogether. But once he decides to bake such cakes for straight customers, the state may forbid him from discriminating against gay customers.

Gorsuch, meanwhile, took an extraordinarily deferential approach to religious objectors. According to Gorsuch, the person raising a religious objection is alone "entitled to define the nature of his religious commitments." And "those commitments, as defined by the faithful adherent, not a bureaucrat or judge, are entitled to protection under the First Amendment."

Gorsuch's approach, in other words, suggests that the only thing necessary for Phillips to gain an exemption from anti-discrimination law—or from many other laws—is for him to claim a religious objection to following that law. The person with the objection gets to define the scope of their own First Amendment rights.

And it is likely that something close to Gorsuch's views in *Masterpiece* will soon become the law of the land. The Court's first major decision after Barrett's confirmation struck down many of New York State's restrictions on the number of people who can attend worship services during the pandemic.

Indeed, a case called *Fulton v. City of Philadelphia* could give religious objectors an even broader ability to press those objections—potentially allowing them to undermine essential government services, and collect significant sums of money from the government in the process.

Fulton presents the question of whether government contractors can refuse to provide the service that they agreed to provide the government, but still get paid under their government contract. The case involves Catholic Social Services (CSS), one of thirty private organizations that contract with the city of Philadelphia to help place children in foster homes. Unlike the other twenty-nine organizations, however, CSS refuses to place foster children with a same-sex couple.

This discrimination against same-sex couples violated CSS's contract with the city, which forbids discrimination on the basis of sexual orientation. Nevertheless, CSS claims that the Constitution's Free Exercise Clause permits it to contract with the city to provide a government service, even if it insists on discriminating against some residents of the city of Philadelphia.

The stakes in *Fulton* are simply enormous. For one thing, the plaintiffs ask the Supreme Court to reconsider—and to potentially overrule—*Employment Division v. Smith*. Recall that, under current Supreme Court precedents, federal laws must comply with the expansive approach to "religious liberty" that the Supreme Court announced in *Hobby Lobby*, but state and local governments may still enforce a "valid and neutral law of general applicability" against religious objectors. If *Smith* is overruled, that would likely extend the *Hobby Lobby* standard to state and local governments as well.

But more than that, *Fulton* could prevent the government from eliminating discrimination even within its own service providers. Whatever you think of Jack Phillips's behavior in *Masterpiece Cakeshop*—or, for that matter, Maurice Bessinger's racism in *Piggie Park*—both cases involved business owners who only had the ability to discriminate within their own private businesses.

Fulton, by contrast, asks the Supreme Court to make the government complicit in one private organization's discrimination. And, if the plaintiffs prevail in that case, their victory could severely undercut the government's ability to provide basic services to all Americans.

Cases like *Fulton* and *Masterpiece Cakeshop* raise other disturbing questions about the future of anti-discrimination law. If the Supreme Court will allow religious objectors to discriminate against LGBTQ individuals, for example, what other kinds of discrimination are permitted?

Justice Alito may have answered this question in *Hobby Lobby*, and the answer appears to be that quite a lot of discrimination will be allowed. In response to Justice Ginsburg's fears that the approach Alito laid out in *Hobby Lobby* would lead to employment discrimination, Alito offered a narrow caveat to his opinion—race discrimination is not permitted. As Alito wrote, "The Government has a compelling interest in providing an equal opportunity to participate in the workforce without

96   regard to race, and prohibitions on racial discrimination are precisely tailored to achieve that critical goal."

So it appears that even Alito would rule against someone like Maurice Bessinger, who claims that religion is a justification for racial discrimination. But what about other forms of discrimination? What about discrimination against LGBTQ workers? Or against women like the married female employees in *Fremont Christian*? By singling out race discrimination in his Hobby Lobby opinion, Alito suggests that other forms of discrimination will be permitted.

Fulton and *Hobby Lobby* suggest that the Supreme Court may allow religious objectors to undercut other government programs as well. Consider the facts of *United States v. Lee*, the case holding that religious business owners must comply with the same laws as their competitors. That case concerned whether someone with religious objections to Social Security could refuse to pay Social Security taxes.

Or consider *Tony & Susan Alamo Foundation v. Secretary of Labor* (1985), which concerned whether an employer may seek a religious objection to minimum wage laws.

In the more permissive regime described in Ryan and Winkler's research, the Supreme Court concluded in both *Lee* and *Tony & Susan Alamo* that religious objectors could not wield those objections to undermine a major federal program, or to defeat wage protections for their workers. If an employer can deny birth control coverage to their employees, despite federal rules requiring the employer to include such coverage in those employees' compensation package, why can't the same employer refuse to pay a minimum wage?

Hobby Lobby, for what it is worth, concluded that it is "untenable to allow individuals to seek exemptions from taxes based on religious objections to particular Government expenditures," so it's likely that Social Security taxes are safe. But *Hobby Lobby* was also decided before Justices Gorsuch, Kavanaugh, and Barrett joined the Court, each shifting the Court dramatically to the right. So there's at least some chance that religious objectors could gain an exemption from at least some taxes.

The Court's "religious liberty" cases are in flux, and it is not at all clear how far the Roberts Court will go in expanding the rights of religious objectors. While it seems likely that these objectors will gain the ability to defy laws prohibiting anti-LGBTQ discrimination, it is not yet clear whether government contractors will gain the right to discriminate. Or whether the Court will reconsider cases like *Lee* and *Tony & Susan Alamo*.

At the very least, however, the Court no longer views claims that religion is a license to discriminate as "patently frivolous," as the Court held in *Piggie Park*. And religious conservatives are likely to gain broad new exemptions from the law in the coming years.

The Right to Sue

Thus far, this book has focused on many of the most consequential cases of our era—lawsuits determining our most important rights, the nature of our democracy, and even more fundamental questions such as the safety of the air we breathe.

We now turn to a case about just $30.22.

The underlying dispute in *AT&T Mobility v. Concepcion* is so insignificant, you may wonder why the case needed to be heard by the Supreme Court at all. A couple purchased cell phone service and were told that they would receive free phones—but they were actually charged $30.22 in sales tax for the phones. They sued, claiming that charging them such a tax on phones advertised as "free" was false advertising and fraud.

But this nothingburger of a case had as much of an impact on the rights of workers and consumers as any other case discussed in this book. In *Concepcion,* and in many cases like it, the Supreme Court has empowered big companies to effectively immunize themselves from many lawsuits—and to drastically reduce their liability in other suits.

In 1925, Congress enacted the Federal Arbitration Act to, in the words of the chairman of the American Bar Association committee that drafted the legislation, "give the merchants the right or the privilege of sitting down and agreeing with each other as to what their damages are, if they want to do it." The idea was that sophisticated businesspeople, when doing business with each other, may prefer arguing their disputes before a private arbitrator who could resolve the case more quickly and less expensively than a judge.

But the Supreme Court has read this 1925 law to permit companies to force their employees and customers to agree to arbitration—and sign away their right to sue the company in a regular court—as a condition of doing business with that company. Research indicates that arbitrators are much more likely to rule in favor of corporate parties than judges, and that arbitrators tend to award less money than courts when a non-corporate plaintiff does prevail.

As one study, which looked at forced arbitration in employment cases, determined, "employee win rates in mandatory arbitration are much lower than in either federal court or state court, with employees in mandatory arbitration winning only just about a fifth of the time (21.4 percent), which is 59 percent as often as in the federal courts and only 38 percent as often as in state courts." Similarly, "the median or typical award in mandatory arbitration" is "only 21 percent of the median award in the federal courts and 43 percent of the median award in the state courts."

And the Supreme Court hasn't simply permitted forced arbitration contracts, it has often twisted the words of the Federal Arbitration Act—or ignored them altogether—in its cases enabling forced arbitration.

The Arbitration Act, for example, specifically exempts "workers engaged in foreign or interstate commerce" from its provisions protecting arbitration contracts. And yet, in *Circuit City v. Adams* (2001), the Supreme Court held that forced arbitration agreements may be enforced against most workers engaged in foreign or interstate commerce.

Similarly, in *Concepcion*, the Supreme Court held that companies may insert a ban on class action lawsuits into forced arbitration agreements, thus giving those companies an additional layer of lawsuit immunity. And that brings us back to the question of why a $30.22 case can matter so much.

Imagine two companies. The first one cheats a single individual out of $300,000. The second company, perhaps gifted with lawyers who are familiar with the Supreme Court's decision in *Concepcion*, cheats ten thousand people out of $30. On paper, both of these companies have exactly $300,000 in ill-gotten gains, but the latter company is on far stronger ground if it is able to avoid class action litigation.

The first company in this hypothetical is likely to get sued, and it is likely to be ordered to return the $300,000 in ill-gotten gains. The company's single victim, moreover, is likely to have an easy time finding a good lawyer because plaintiffs' lawyers typically are paid a percentage of their client's winnings—and a $300,000 case is valuable enough that the lawyer who brings it can expect to walk away with a good payday.

Class actions allow multiple plaintiffs with similar cases against the same defendant to all join together under the banner of a single lawsuit. So, if the ten thousand victims of the second company are able to bring a class action suit, they should also be able to find a good lawyer willing to represent them. But if class actions are forbidden, that would mean that each one of these ten thousand individuals will have to bring their own $30 lawsuit.

Not only is no lawyer likely to take a $30 case, but the potential plaintiffs are likely to decide that a $30 dispute isn't worth the effort. As one federal judge argued in a similar context, "the *realistic* alternative to a class action is not 17 million individual suits, but zero individual suits, as only a lunatic or a fanatic sues for $30."

Concepcion, in other words, allows many companies to break the law without consequence, so long as they only target individuals a few dollars at a time. A company that refuses to pay a single worker $50,000 is likely to be sued. But a company that cheats each of its two hundred workers out of $250 will likely get off scot free, so long as it requires those workers to sign a forced arbitration contract with a class action ban. The cost of winning a $250 case is likely to be much greater than $250, so it's not worth the effort to bring that case in the first place.

So, while they receive far less attention than many of the Court's other cases, and while the Court's forced arbitration cases often dwell on hypertechnical issues, they are among the most consequential cases decided by the Supreme Court. What use is a right to be safe from fraud, or to be paid a minimum wage, or to be free from discrimination, if these rights cannot be meaningfully enforced?

The Supreme Court's Arbitration Decisions Take Tremendous Liberty with the Law's Text

The Supreme Court's decisions permitting forced arbitration often emphasize that courts must apply "a liberal federal policy favoring arbitration agreements, notwithstanding any state substantive or procedural policies to the contrary." In practice, the Supreme Court has taken such a favorable position toward arbitration that its arbitration decisions are hard to square with the law's explicit text.

Consider *Circuit City*, which held that employers may use forced arbitration in most employment contracts. In practice, many employers make agreeing to forced arbitration a condition of employment—meaning that a worker who refuses to sign away their right to sue is immediately terminated.

But the Arbitration Act explicitly excludes employment contracts from the "liberal federal policy favoring arbitration agreements" that the Court loves to tout. Forced arbitration should not exist at all in the workplace.

Circuit City turned on the meaning of a very important word that appears twice in the Federal Arbitration Act—the word "commerce." One provision of the Arbitration Act provides that written arbitration agreements found in "a contract evidencing a transaction involving commerce" are "valid, irrevocable, and enforceable, save upon such grounds as exist at law or in equity for the revocation of any contract." A second provision excludes "contracts of employment of seamen, railroad employees, or any other class of workers engaged in foreign or interstate commerce" from this broader policy favoring arbitration contracts.

Recall that, at the time when the Arbitration Act was enacted, the Supreme Court defined the word "commerce" very narrowly. Just seven years before the Arbitration Act became law, the Supreme Court handed down *Hammer v. Dagenhart* (1918), its infamous child labor decision, holding that the word "commerce" encompassed only the "transportation" of goods, and not the "manufacture" of those goods.

Thus, in 1925, when the Arbitration Act became law, Congress understood the word "commerce" to only include transit of goods for sale, and perhaps the sale of the goods themselves. The production of those goods, through manufacturing, agriculture, mining, or similar means—as well as the labor that went into such production—was not considered to be "commerce" in 1925.

So when Congress wrote that the Arbitration Act applies to any "contract evidencing a transaction involving commerce," it meant that nearly all employment contracts were not covered by the Act. After all, under the 1925 understanding of the word "commerce," employment contracts involving factory workers, farmhands, miners, and countless other workers did not count as a contract "involving commerce."

Similarly, when the 1925 Congress wrote that "contracts of employment of seamen, railroad employees, or any other class of workers engaged in foreign or interstate commerce," it intended to exclude all employment contracts from the Federal Arbitration Act's scope. We know this because, in 1925, the phrase "contracts of employment of seamen, railroad employees, or any other class of workers engaged in foreign or interstate commerce" would have encompassed all workers engaged in "transportation," the only activity that counted as "commerce" under decisions like *Hammer*—and thus the only kind of employment contract that Congress plausibly could have brought within the Arbitration Act's reach in 1925.

But *Circuit City* rejected this history, and it held that the word "commerce" has two entirely different meanings when it is used in two different places within the Arbitration Act.

The Court held that, when the Arbitration Act defines its scope—stating that the Act applies to all written arbitration

104   contracts "involving commerce"—the word "commerce" must
        be read very broadly. In this context, the Court claimed, the
        word "commerce" must be read as "implementing Congress'
        intent 'to exercise [its] commerce power to the full.'" That is,
        the Arbitration Act must be read to apply to any contract that
        fits within the Court's modern, expansive understanding of the
        word "commerce"—an understanding that is expansive enough
        to encompass nearly all employment contracts.

            And yet, the Court also read the provision protecting "sea-
        men, railroad employees, or any other class of workers engaged
        in foreign or interstate commerce" very narrowly. In this con-
        text, *Circuit City* claims the word "commerce" applies only to
        "transportation workers."

            Circuit City, in other words, applied the modern definition
        of the word "commerce" to one provision of the Arbitration Act,
        and the 1925 definition of the same word to a different provision
        of the same Act. This is, to put it mildly, not how courts typi-
        cally interpret laws. As the Supreme Court explained in a dif-
        ferent context, a term that appears multiple times in the same
        statute should presumptively "be construed, if possible, to give
        it a consistent meaning throughout the Act."

            Concepcion, which held that forced arbitration agreements
        may also require individuals to sign away their right to bring a
        class action, takes similar liberties with the text of the Arbitra-
        tion Act.

            Recall that the Arbitration Act provides that arbitra-
        tion contracts are "valid, irrevocable, and enforceable, save
        upon such grounds as exist at law or in equity for the revoca-
        tion of any contract." California law banned many "class action
        waivers" altogether, regardless of whether that waiver appeared

in an arbitration agreement or not. So California's ban on class action waivers should have applied to forced arbitration agreements that also prohibit class actions. The Arbitration Act prohibits states from discriminating against arbitration agreements. It does not prevent them from enforcing universal contracting laws that apply equally to all contracts.

The Arbitration Act, moreover, makes no mention of class action lawsuits. There is no provision of that Act that suggests, or even hints, that Congress intended to allow companies to dodge class action suits when it enacted the Arbitration Act. Nevertheless, *Concepcion* held that the right of companies to impose class action bans on their workers and consumers may be found within penumbras and emanations of the Arbitration Act.

Rather than follow the text of the Arbitration Act, *Concepcion* relied on several policy-based objections to permitting class actions in arbitration. Class arbitration, Justice Scalia wrote for the Court, moves slower than one-on-one arbitration—often taking years to resolve rather than a matter of mere months. It requires greater procedural formality than ordinary arbitration, and it "greatly increases risks to defendants," because a defendant who loses big in class arbitration typically has no way to appeal that decision.

These policy-based arguments all offer reasons why a legislator, who believes that arbitration is superior to litigation, might push to amend the Arbitration Act to limit class actions in arbitration. But it is not the job of a court to cure policy defects it perceives in a federal statute. And it certainly isn't the job of a court to decide that certain values—speedy resolution of disputes, procedural informality, low risk for corporate parties—are paramount over other values, such as ensuring that workers and consumers can vindicate their legal rights.

Concepcion, by contrast, starts with the premise that there must be a "federal policy favoring arbitration," and then reasons backward to achieve that policy goal, even when doing so means ignoring the text of the Arbitration Act.

All the Laws but One

Justice Gorsuch won rare praise from the civil rights community for his decision in *Bostock v. Clayton County* (2020), which held that the Civil Rights Act of 1964's ban on "sex" discrimination encompasses discrimination on the basis of sexual orientation and gender identity.

Bostock was a triumph of "textualism," the belief that statutory interpretation should begin and end with the text of a statute, and that policy concerns or concerns about how Congress intended that statute to function are irrelevant. Gorsuch is the Supreme Court's most outspoken evangelist of textualism, which he has said is "about ensuring that our written law is our actual law."

There's no doubt that the lawmakers who enacted the Civil Rights Act in the mid-1960s did not believe that they were banning discrimination against LGBTQ Americans. Among other things, the federal government deemed gay people to be "unsuitable for Federal employment" when the Civil Rights Act became law.

And yet, to his credit, Gorsuch followed his textualist approach to statutory interpretation in *Bostock* even though it meant ignoring the intentions of the 1964 Congress, and even though it meant setting aside Gorsuch's conservative policy preferences. As he explained, a statutory ban on "sex" discrimination unavoidably encompasses discrimination against LGBTQ workers:

> Consider, for example, an employer with two employees, both of whom are attracted to men. The two individuals are, to the employer's mind, materially identical in all respects, except that one is a man and the other a woman. If the employer fires the male employee for no reason other than the fact he is attracted to men, the employer discriminates against him for traits or actions it tolerates in his female colleague.

Similarly, if an employer "fires a transgender person who was identified as a male at birth but who now identifies as a female," but also "retains an otherwise identical employee who was identified as female at birth, the employer intentionally penalizes a person identified as male at birth for traits or actions that it tolerates in an employee identified as female at birth."

Yet, while Gorsuch's allegiance to textualism overcame his conservative politics in *Bostock*, the Court's most outspoken textualist abandoned this approach to statutory interpretation when the Arbitration Act was in play.

Gorsuch's first major decision after joining the Supreme Court was his majority opinion in *Epic Systems v. Lewis* (2018), and that decision encapsulates all of the atextual pathologies of the Court's arbitration decisions. *Epic Systems* involved employers that, as Justice Ginsburg explained in dissent, required their employees to "sign, as a condition of employment, arbitration agreements banning collective judicial and arbitral proceedings of any kind."

Thus, *Epic Systems* effectively merged the Court's previous decisions in *Circuit City* and *Concepcion*. Because of *Circuit City*'s atextual interpretation of the Arbitration Act, employers are allowed to force arbitration agreements upon their workers under pain of termination. And, because of *Concepcion*'s atextual interpretation of the same law, those employers may also forbid their employees from joining together in a class action or a similar form of collective legal proceeding.

But there was also an additional wrinkle in *Epic Systems*. A second statute, the National Labor Relations Act (NLRA), provides that workers have the right to form unions, to bargain collectively, and to "engage in other concerted activities for the purpose of collective bargaining or other mutual aid or protection." Class actions and other collective legal proceedings are a kind of "concerted activity" that workers can engage in for their own "mutual aid or protection," because they involve multiple workers banding together under the same lawsuit in order to preserve their collective rights.

So there were three good textualist reasons why workers should have prevailed in *Epic Systems*. First, contrary to *Circuit City*, the Arbitration Act exempts "workers engaged in foreign or interstate commerce" from its provisions. Second, contrary to *Concepcion*, nothing in the text of the Arbitration Act shields contracts prohibiting collective legal proceedings. And third, even if the Court felt compelled to follow its prior erroneous precedents, the NLRA provides another, independent reason why workers should still be able to bring collective actions against their employers.

And yet, Gorsuch was unmoved by these textualist reasons why the workers should have prevailed in *Epic Systems*. Much of his reasoning in that case, moreover, relied on ideas about the role of contracts in the workplace that the Supreme Court abandoned with the end of the *Lochner* Era.

Gorsuch's opinion begins with two rhetorical questions: "Should employees and employers be allowed to agree that any disputes between them will be resolved through one-on-one arbitration? Or should employees always be permitted to bring their claims in class or collective actions, no matter what they agreed with their employers?"—the implication being that workers can meaningfully consent to sign away their rights even when they are ordered to give up those rights or else be fired.

But, as Ginsburg explains in dissent, the entire purpose of the NLRA was to prevent employers from forcing workers into signing away important legal rights. A common device in the *Lochner* Era was the "yellow-dog contract." "Such agreements," Ginsburg writes, "which employers required employees to sign as a condition of employment, typically commanded employees to abstain from joining labor unions."

But the NLRA effectively outlawed yellow-dog contracts, as well as other workplace agreements that strip workers of their ability to band together for their own "mutual aid or protection." Congress understood that federal legislation was necessary to "redress the bargaining power imbalance workers faced." *Epic Systems* effectively undoes this aspect of the NLRA, by legalizing a form of exploitative contract that Congress invalidated.

The implications of this decision are simply breathtaking, and they potentially overwhelm the gains workers enjoy from decisions such as *Bostock*. After all, what good is a right to be free from employment discrimination if your employer can force you to sign that right away—or, at least, if your employer can shunt any disputes raised by its workers into a privatized arbitration system that tends to favor corporate parties?

What use is a minimum wage, or a right to not be charged hidden fees, or even a right not to be physically harmed by a defective product, if those rights cannot be vindicated in court?

Conclusion

In writing this book, I've strived to avoid unnecessary specu-
lation and to keep a measured tone. I suspect that, with a 6—3
Republican majority, the Supreme Court will be extraordinarily aggressive in moving the law to the right. Rather than
guess at how the Court will do so, however, I've tried to focus on
the specific issues that have recently been before the Court, or
that the justices themselves have shown a particular interest in
resolving.

But let me end this book with a note of alarm. The four
issues discussed in this book—voting rights, administrative
law, religion, and forced arbitration—aren't necessarily the
most high-profile issues that reach the Court. But they share a
common theme. They are structural issues that shape the most
important questions in any system of law. Which rights can be
meaningfully enforced? Who is beyond the reach of the law? Is
the government fully empowered to govern?

And the most important question of all: Who makes the
laws that most of us must obey?

Two weeks after Justice Ruth Bader Ginsburg's death, the Supreme Court announced that it would hear a pair of cases— *Brnovich v. Democratic National Committee* and *Arizona Republican Party v. Democratic National Committee*—that could potentially allow the Supreme Court to drive the final nail in the Voting Rights Act's coffin. At the very least, the Supreme Court is likely to use these cases, which ask whether the Voting Rights Act invalidates two Arizona laws restricting the right to vote, to further weaken protections against racist voting laws.

In a world without a vibrant Voting Rights Act, it's far from clear that the Democratic Party's multiracial coalition will remain competitive at the national level. Without strong protections against racial voting discrimination, red states are likely to enact a wave of laws targeting Black and brown voters, gerrymandering those voters into packed districts, and reallocating election resources to force voters of color to wait hours to cast a ballot. Worse, if the Supreme Court embraces the radical theory that only the state legislature may decide how the state conducts federal elections, Democratic governors could lose their power to veto voter suppression bills, and state supreme courts could lose their ability to protect the right to vote.

Over time, much of the Democratic Party's diverse base will find it harder and harder to vote. Many of these voters will give up. Democrats will no doubt still dominate liberal states like New York and California. But they will struggle more and more with each passing election to win the Congress or the presidency—especially if unchecked gerrymandering allows Republicans to dominate US House elections in swing states.

This vicious cycle has begun, and it will be very difficult to reverse. If Democrats cannot win national elections, they

cannot enact new voting rights laws, and they cannot appoint
new justices who might shift the Court back toward the center.

The Supreme Court's 6–3 Republican majority is potentially an existential threat to the Democratic Party's national ambitions—and, more importantly, to liberal democracy in the United States.

It's also worth restating that the Supreme Court became such a threat to American democracy thanks to a system of government that allowed a political party that most Americans do not support to stack the Court with loyal conservatives.

In 2012, President Obama won reelection, receiving a majority of all ballots cast. Moreover, while Democrats lost control of the Senate in the 2014 midterms, they lost Congress's upper house because the Senate effectively gives extra representation to conservative white voters.

In the GOP Senate that blocked Obama Supreme Court nominee Merrick Garland's confirmation in 2016, Democratic senators represented about twenty million more people than their Republican counterparts. Garland is not a justice today because the Senate gives red Wyoming exactly the same number of senators as blue California, despite the fact that California has over sixty-eight times as many people as Wyoming.

Unlike Obama, Donald Trump lost the popular vote in 2016, and Republicans held onto the Senate thanks to malapportionment. Yet Trump was able to appoint three justices.

Republicans, in other words, control the Supreme Court because of an anti-democratic system that effectively makes Republican voters count more than Democratic voters. And Republicans are now poised to use their control of the Supreme Court to skew our elections even more deeply in favor of the GOP.

I do not read much legal theory—or, at least, I do not read much legal theory that is not written by judges or justices. In my experience, if you want to understand why the Supreme Court has acted the way it acted in the past, or if you want to make thoughtful predictions about how it will act in the future, you are better off studying history and politics than the kind of law review articles that use words like "heuristic" or "orthogonal."

That said, if you read just one work of legal theory, it should be John Hart Ely's *Democracy and Distrust: A Theory of Judicial Review*. The most significant Supreme Court case of the twentieth century, and one of the Court's best attempts to make sense of our vague Constitution, is the Court's decision in *United States v. Carolene Products* (1938). Briefly, *Carolene Products* held that courts should typically defer to elected officials, except when those elected officials target the democratic process itself—such as through voter disenfranchisement or by excluding the voices of disfavored minorities.

Ely's masterwork builds his theory of the role of courts in our society off of *Carolene Products'* insight. The judiciary, Ely argues, should exist to enhance democracy. It should be highly reluctant to exercise power *except* when the ability of voters to shape their government is threatened—and then it should be highly aggressive. Close readers of Ely will notice that he and I do not agree on everything. I view a dynamic administrative state as an essential part of a modern democracy, while he tends to be more skeptical. But his overarching vision, which sees judges as the referees that allow the game of democracy to be played forever, is an inspired one.

If you read a second work of legal theory, it should be Justice Antonin Scalia's *A Matter of Interpretation: Federal Courts and the Law*. Scalia's book is an unusual one, in that it features a fairly short essay on the role of judges by Scalia himself, and then several responses from scholars critiquing Scalia's essay. Whatever else can be said about Justice Scalia, he was a man of extraordinary intellectual confidence. And he was happy to present his arguments alongside those of his detractors.

In any event, I specifically want to recommend Scalia's own essay. I certainly do not agree with every point that Scalia makes. But the late justice argues persuasively that judicial power—which, after all, is exercised by the one unelected branch of government—is dangerous to our democracy if left unchecked. *A Matter of Interpretation* is a relic of an era when conservatives still feared judicial power and believed that judges needed to follow a set of rules and principles that would limit such power. I only wish that they still felt the same way today.

The best work of legal history that I know of is Michael Klarman's *From Jim Crow to Civil Rights: The Supreme Court and the Struggle for Racial Equality*. Klarman's book is a work about the Supreme Court, but it is just as much a book about the terroristic violence at the heart of the South's white supremacist regime. Decisions like *Brown v. Board of Education* accelerated the movement towards civil rights, not because this regime respected the Court's decision, but because white supremacists responded to *Brown* with such unconcealed violence that northerners could no longer look away from it.

On the subject of voting rights in particular, several excellent—and fairly recent—books chronicle the history of voter suppression in the United States and the reemergence of Jim Crow—style tactics in the last decade. They include Carol Anderson's *One Person, No Vote: How Voter Suppression Is Destroying Our Democracy*, Ari Berman's *Give Us the Ballot: The Modern Struggle for Voting Rights in America*, and Michael Waldman's *The Fight to Vote*. I found each of these books helpful in getting my own head around the kinds of tactics that illiberal movements within the United States have always used to restrict the franchise.

Finally, Thomas Mann and Norm Ornstein's *It's Even Worse Than It Looks: How the American Constitutional System Collided with the New Politics of Extremism* is an invaluable exploration of why the US constitutional system, which depends on compromise to function, is so vulnerable to a political movement that disdains such compromise. Mann and Ornstein were pillars of Washington, DC's centrist establishment for many years, so their book is particularly notable for its willingness to lay blame at the fect of the Republican Party.

If the United States is to emerge from this era of acrimony and non-governance, then we must evolve towards a constitutional system that fears dysfunction at least as much as it fears government action. We must have a Court that does not confuse stagnation with liberty. And, above all, we must have a Senate that does not treat a voter in Wyoming as sixty-eight times more valuable than a voter in California.

INTRODUCTION

8   dismantled much of America's campaign finance law: See *McCutcheon v. Fed. Election Comm'n*, 572 U.S. 185, 192 (2014) ("[G]overnment regulation may not target the general gratitude a candidate may feel toward those who support him or his allies, or the political access such support may afford."); *Arizona Free Enterprise Club's Freedom Club PAC v. Bennett*, 564 U.S. 721, 728–29 (2011) (dismissing a law intended to protect a public financing scheme as an unconstitutional "government effort[] to increase the speech of some at the expense of others").

8   severely weakened the Voting Rights Act: See *Abbott v. Perez*, 138 S. Ct. 2305, 2325 (2018) (granting an extraordinarily high "presumption of legislative good faith" to lawmakers accused of racial voter discrimination); *Shelby Cnty. v. Holder*, 570 U.S. 529, 557 (2013) (striking down §4(b) of the Voting Rights Act).

8   permitted states to opt out of the Affordable Care Act's Medicaid expansion: *Nat'l Fed'n of Indep. Bus. v. Sebelius*, 567 U.S. 519, 581 (2012) (describing the Affordable Care Act's Medicaid expansion as a "gun to the head" of the states).

8   permitting someone who objects to the law on religious grounds: See *Burwell v. Hobby Lobby Stores, Inc.*, 134 S. Ct. 2751, 2759 (2014) (holding that businesses with religious objections to birth control may ignore federal rules requiring them to provide contraception coverage to their employees); *id.* at 2787 (Ginsburg, J., dissenting) ("In the Court's view, RFRA demands accommodation of a for-profit corporation's religious beliefs no matter the impact that accommodation may have on third parties who do not share the corporation owners' religious faith.)

8   weakened laws shielding workers from sexual and racial harassment: See *Vance v. Ball State Univ*, 570 U.S. 421, 429 (2013) (weakening protections against harassment by a supervisor).

8   into a privatized arbitration system: See *Epic Sys. Corp. v. Lewis*, 138 S. Ct. 1612, 1632 (2018) (permitting employers to force their workers to give up their right to sue the employer, shunt disputes between the worker and the company into privatized arbitration, and require those workers to give up their right to bring a class action).

8   undercut public sector unions' ability to raise funds: See *Janus v. Am. Fed'n of State, Cnty., & Mun. Emps.*, Council 31, 138 S. Ct. 2448, 2460 (2018) (prohibiting public sector unions from charging "agency fees" to non-union members who benefit from the union's services).

8 **effectively eliminated the president's recess appointments power:** See *Nat'l Labor Relations Bd. v. Noel Canning*, 134 S. Ct. 2550, 2556–57 (2014) (permitting the Senate to effectively eliminate the president's recess appointments power by holding brief "*pro forma*" sessions).

8 **halted President Obama's Clean Power Plan:** *West Virginia v. EPA*, 135 S.Ct. 1000, 1000 (2016).

9 **held that every state must permit same-sex couples to marry:** *Obergefell v. Hodges*, 135 S. Ct. 2584, 2604–05 (2015).

9 **prohibits employers from firing individuals because of their sexual orientation or gender identity:** *Bostock v. Clayton Cty.*, 207 L. Ed. 2d 218, 230 (2020).

9 **less likely to enact legislation overriding a Supreme Court decision:** Rick Hasen, "End of the Dialogue? Political Polarization, the Supreme Court, and Congress," *S. Calif. L. Rev.* 86 (2013), 101, 154.

9 **"an average of twelve overrides of Supreme Court cases":** Rick Hasen, "End of the Dialogue? Political Polarization, the Supreme Court, and Congress," 105.

9 **That number shrunk to 5.8 overrides:** Rick Hasen, "End of the Dialogue? Political Polarization, the Supreme Court, and Congress," 105.   117

10 **"partisanship seems to have strongly diminished the opportunities for bipartisan overrides":** Rick Hasen, "End of the Dialogue? Political Polarization, the Supreme Court, and Congress," 105.

10 **that decision can only be overruled by the Supreme Court itself:** See *Marbury v. Madison*, 5 U.S. (1 Cranch) 137, 178 (1803) ("the courts are to regard the constitution, and the constitution is superior to any ordinary act of the legislature . . .").

11 **judges who "impose their social and political viewpoints upon the American people":** Ian Millhiser, *Injustices: The Supreme Court's History of Comforting the Comfortable and Afflicting the Afflicted* (2015), 203.

11 **warned of judges who "give in to temptation and make law instead of interpreting":** Ian Millhiser, "How Conservatives Abandoned Judicial Restraint, Took Over the Courts and Radically Transformed America," Think Progress (November 19, 2013) at https://thinkprogress.org /how-conservatives-abandoned -judicial-restraint-took-over-the -courts-and-radically-transformed -3da3115c81c0/.

118

11 **"the claim for judicial modesty is sufficiently well-established":** Ian Millhiser, "How Conservatives Abandoned Judicial Restraint, Took Over the Courts and Radically Transformed America."

11 **future justice Neil Gorsuch denounced "American liberals" who "have become addicted to the courtroom":** Neil Gorsuch, "Liberals'N'Lawsuits," *National Review* (February 7, 2005) at https://www.nationalreview.com/2005/02/liberalsnlawsuits-joseph-6/.

11 **called for the judiciary to claim a broad new power to veto federal regulations:** See *Gundy v. United States,* 139 S.Ct. 2116, 2135–37 (2019) (Gorsuch, J., dissenting) (laying out a vague new test that courts should use to strike down federal regulation).

11–12 **argued that courts should give Christian conservatives broad exemptions:** See *Masterpiece Cakeshop, Ltd. v. Colo. Civil Rights Comm'n,* 138 S. Ct. 1719, 1739 (2018) (Gorsuch, J., concurring) (arguing that courts should give broad deference to religious objectors seeking an exemption from the law). Though Gorsuch has been extraordinarily sympathetic to conservative Christians raising "religious liberty" claims, he's been far less sympathetic to people of other faiths. See, e.g., *Dunn v. Ray,* 139 S. Ct. 661, 661 (2019) (permitting a Muslim inmate to be executed without his spiritual adviser present, even though a Christian inmate would have been allowed to have such an adviser present); *Trump v. Hawaii,* 138 S. Ct. 2392, 2419–20 (2018) (holding that the president is entitled to great deference when preventing foreign nationals from traveling to the United States, even when there is considerable evidence that the president was motivated by anti-Muslim animus).

12 **suggested that the Court should revive an antiquated "freedom of contract" doctrine:** *Sveen v. Melin,* 138 S. Ct. 1815 (2018) (Gorsuch, J., dissenting) ("[A]ny legislative deviation from a contract's obligations, 'however minute, or apparently immaterial,' violates the Constitution." (quoting *Green v. Biddle,* 8 Wheat. 1, 84, 5 L.Ed. 547 (1823)).

12 **forcing states with voucher programs to provide such vouchers to religious schools:** *Espinoza v. Montana Dept. of Revenue,* 140 S. Ct. 2246, 2261 (2020).

12 **"If you ask me where American aristocracy is found":** Alexis de Tocqueville, *Democracy in America* (Penguin Classics, 2003), 313.

12 **"are secretly opposed to the instincts of democracy":** Alexis de Tocqueville, *Democracy in America,* 313.

13   it took only six days to make the same journey across the United States: Ian Millhiser, "How Conservatives Abandoned Judicial Restraint, Took Over the Courts and Radically Transformed America," 20.

13   Industrialization transformed America: Ian Millhiser, "How Conservatives Abandoned Judicial Restraint, Took Over the Courts and Radically Transformed America," 8, 45.

13   In a pre-industrial America, local businesses served local customers: Ian Millhiser, "How Conservatives Abandoned Judicial Restraint, Took Over the Courts and Radically Transformed America," 46–47.

14   told that organization in an 1881 address: Report on the Fourth Annual Meeting of the American Bar Association, American Bar Association (1881), 172.

14   typical of the views of many elite lawyers in the early industrial era: Report on the Fourth Annual Meeting of the American Bar Association, 172–73.

15   every great corporation within its reach prepares for self-defense: "The Outlook," Am. J. of Politics 5 (1894), 440, 442.

15   who argued that judges should impose strict constitutional limits: Christopher

G. Tiedeman, A Treatise on State and Federal Control of Persons and Property in the United States Considered from Both a Civil and Criminal Standpoint (1900), ix.

15–16   urged courts to "lay their interdict upon all legislative acts": Christopher G. Tiedeman, The Unwritten Constitution of the United States: A Philosophical Inquiry into the Fundamentals of American Constitutional Law (1890), 80–81.

16   the Supreme Court's decision in Lochner v. New York: 198 U.S. 45 (1905).

16   struck down a New York law limiting the amount of time: 198 U.S. 45.

16   "unnecessary and arbitrary interference with the right of the individual": 198 U.S. 56.

16   "the liberty of contract relating to labor includes both parties to it": 198 U.S. 56.

16   would rely on Lochner to strike down minimum wage laws: Adkins v. Children's Hospital of DC, 261 U.S. 525, 560–62 (1923).

16   to strike down laws protecting workers' right to join a union: Adair v. United States, 208 U.S. 161, 174 (1908).

16–17   "it is not within the functions of government," the Court held in Adair v. United States: 208 U.S. 161 (1908).

120

17 **few bakers earned more than $12 a week:** Ian Millhiser, "How Conservatives Abandoned Judicial Restraint, Took Over the Courts and Radically Transformed America," 93.

17 **were frequently built in the basements of tenements:** "Tenth Annual Report of the Factory Inspectors of the State of New York," *Documents of the Assembly of the State of New York* 11 (1896), 52–53.

17 **"Filth, cobwebs and vermin" abounded in these basement bakeries:** "Tenth Annual Report of the Factory Inspectors of the State of New York," 52–54.

18 **workers were forced not just to work, but to sleep in these conditions:** "Tenth Annual Report of the Factory Inspectors of the State of New York," 53.

18 **the price of these makeshift accommodations were deducted from their wages:** Ian Millhiser, "How Conservatives Abandoned Judicial Restraint, Took Over the Courts and Radically Transformed America," 93.

18 **"The employer and the employe [sic] have equality of right":** 208 U.S. 161, 175 (1908).

18 **the Court spent much of Roosevelt's first term striking down New Deal policies:** See Ian Millhiser, "How Conservatives Abandoned Judicial Restraint, Took Over the Courts And Radically Transformed America," 135–57 (describing Roosevelt's fight with the Supreme Court).

18 **"[e]mployees shall have the right to self-organization":** 29 U.S.C. § 157 (1935).

19 **Nor were the lawmakers who drafted the NLRA shy about their disdain:** 29 U.S.C. at § 151.

19 **struck down a law prohibiting goods produced by child laborers:** 247 U.S. 251 (1918).

19 **to "regulate commerce . . . among the several states":** U.S. Const. Art. I, Sec. 8.

20 **because the purpose of the child labor law at issue in** *Hammer***:** 247 U.S. at 272–73.

20 **abandoned this narrow vision of federal power and upheld the NLRA:** 301 U.S. 1 (1937).

20 **that it makes no sense for the courts to draw a line between manufacturing and commerce:** 301 U.S. 37.

20 **can have "a most serious effect upon interstate commerce":** 301 U.S. 41.

20 **A year later, in** *United States v. Carolene Products***:** 304 U.S. 144 (1938).

20 **in somewhat needlessly turgid prose:** 304 U.S. 152–53.

21 In a famous footnote, Stone then listed several cases: 304 U.S. 153 n4.

21–22 On the eve of oral arguments in *NFIB v. Sebelius*: 132 S. Ct. 2566 (2012).

22 an American Bar Association poll of Supreme Court experts: Jon Healey, "Legal Experts Predict a Supreme Court Win for 'Obamacare,'" *Los Angeles Times*, March 14, 2012, at https: //opinion.latimes.com/opinionla /2012/03/poll-of-legal-experts -predicts-a-win-for-obamacare .html.

22 four justices voted to repeal the Affordable Care Act in its entirety: *NFIB*, 132 S.Ct. at 2677.

22 initially voted to strike down several key provisions of the law: Joan Biskupic, "The Inside Story of How John Roberts Negotiated to Save Obamacare," CNN, March 25, 2019, at https://www.cnn .com/2019/03/21/politics /john-roberts-obamacare-the -chief/index.html.

22 Yale law professor Jack Balkin writes: Jack Balkin, "Why Liberals and Conservatives Flipped on Judicial Restraint: Judicial Review in the Cycles of Constitutional Time," *Texas L. Rev.* 98 (2019), 215, 219.

23 tends to embrace a rhetoric of judicial restraint: Jack Balkin, "Why Liberals and Conservatives Flipped on Judicial Restraint: Judicial Review in the Cycles of Constitutional Time," 220.

23 "may cling to their long-held beliefs about judicial review": Jack Balkin, "Why Liberals and Conservatives Flipped on Judicial Restraint: Judicial Review in the Cycles of Constitutional Time," 220.

23 Gorsuch was five years old on the day that the Supreme Court handed down *Roe v. Wade*: 410 U.S. 113 (1973).

24 to suggest that the Court was correct to strike down child labor laws: Concurring in *United States v. Lopez*, Justice Thomas argued that the Constitution's Commerce Clause, as originally understood, does not encompass "activities such as manufacturing and agriculture." 514 U.S. 549, 586 (1995) (Thomas, J., concurring). This is the same reasoning that the Court used in 1918 to invalidate federal child labor laws. See *Hammer v. Dagenhart*, 247 U.S. 251, 273–74 (1918) ("The grant of power to Congress over the subject of interstate commerce was to enable it to regulate such commerce, and not to give it authority to control the States in their exercise of the police power over local trade and manufacture.")

24 in order to restore the "original understanding":

122 *Lopez,* 514 U.S. at 584 (Thomas, J., concurring).

24 **the only conservative justice who has never joined his liberal colleagues:** Ian Millhiser, "What Happens to the Supreme Court (and the Constitution) if Trump Wins," Vox, August 25, 2020, at https://www.vox.com/2020/7/21/21328863/supreme-court-trump-vacancy-voting-rights-rnc2020-epa-police. The one plausible exception to Alito's unbroken record is his brief concurring opinion in *Gundy v. United States.* But, in *Gundy,* Alito endorsed a conservative deregulatory project that is rejected by all of the Court's liberals. 139 S. Ct. 2116, 2131 (2019) (Alito, J., concurring in the judgment).

25 **wrote the Supreme Court's decision in *Shelby County v. Holder:*** 133 S.Ct. 2612 (2013).

25 **wrote opinions like *McCutcheon v. Federal Election Commission:*** 134 S.Ct. 1434 (2014).

25 **Roberts rejects a wholesale return to *Lochner:*** See *Obergefell v. Hodges* 135 S.Ct. 2584, 2616 (2015) (Roberts, C.J., dissenting) (describing *Lochner* as a "discredited" decision).

26 **the right to vote is "preservative of all rights":** *Yick Wo v. Hopkins,* 118 U.S. 356, 370 (1886).

26 **has been unusually hostile to voting rights:** 553 U.S. 181 (2008).

26 **prohibiting laws that impose restrictions on the right to vote:** See 553 U.S. 209 (Souter, J., dissenting) ([A] State may not burden the right to vote merely by invoking abstract interests . . . but must make a particular, factual showing that threats to its interests outweigh the particular impediments it has imposed. The State has made no such justification here, and as to some aspects of its law, it has hardly even tried.")

26 **required states and localities with a history of racial voter suppression:** *Shelby Cnty. v. Holder,* 570 U.S. 529, 557 (2013).

26 **in *Abbott v. Perez:*** 138 S. Ct. 2305 (2018).

26 **it may no longer be possible for such plaintiffs to prevail:** See 138 S. Ct. 2325 (granting an extraordinarily high "presumption of legislative good faith" to lawmakers accused of racial voter discrimination).

26 **undercutting our regulation of campaign finance:** See *McCutcheon v. Fed. Election Comm'n,* 572 U.S. 185, 192 (2014) ("[G]overnment regulation may not target the general gratitude a candidate may feel toward those who support him or his allies, or the political access such support may afford."); *Arizona Free*

Enterprise Club's Freedom Club PAC v. Bennett, 564 U.S. 721, 728–29 (2011) (dismissing a law intended to protect a public financing scheme as an unconstitutional "government effort . . . to increase the speech of some at the expense of others").

26 **permitting partisan gerrymandering to go unchecked:** *Rucho v. Common Cause*, 139 S. Ct. 2484, 2506–07 (2019).

26 **defunding much of the Democratic Party's political infrastructure:** *Janus v. American Federation of State*, 138 S. Ct. 2448, 2460 (2018) (striking down a major funding source for public sector unions).

27 **And the third is Amy Coney Barrett, Trump's third:** Ian Millhiser, "How an Anti-Democratic Constitution Gave America Amy Coney Barrett," Vox, October 26, 2020, at https://www .vox.com/2020/10/26/21534358 /supreme-court-amy-coney -barrett-constitution-anti -democratic-electoral-college -senate.

27 **the Federalist Society, which played an outsized role:** Ian Millhiser, "Trump Says He Will Delegate Judicial Selection to the Conservative Federalist Society," Think Progress, June 15, 2016, at https://archive.thinkprogress.org /trump-says-he-will-delegate -judicial-selection-to-the

-conservative-federalist-society -26f622b10c49/.

27 **proposals to strip federal agencies of their ability:** Ian Millhiser, "The Little-Noticed Conservative Plan to Permanently Lock Democrats Out of Policymaking," Think Progress, November 16, 2015, at https: //archive.thinkprogress.org /the-little-noticed-conservative -plan-to-permanently-lock -democrats-out-of-policymaking -9f776ad16635/.

27 **became an "unspoken litmus test":** David A. Kaplan, *The Most Dangerous Branch: Inside the Supreme Court in the Age of Trump* (2018), 42.

28 **broad new veto power over federal agencies:** Ian Millhiser, "Brett Kavanaugh's Latest Opinion Should Terrify Democrats," Vox, November 26, 2019, at https://www.vox .com/2019/11/26/20981758/brett -kavanaughs-terrify-democrats -supreme-court-gundy-paul.

28 **As the Supreme Court held in** *United States v. Lee:* 455 U.S. 252 (1982).

28 **enter into commercial activity as a matter of choice:** 455 U.S. 261.

28 **held for the first time, in** *Burwell v. Hobby Lobby:* 134 S.Ct. 2751 (2014).

124   28   **may invoke their faith to limit the rights of a third party:** 134 S.Ct. 2759 (holding that religious business owners could deny birth control coverage to their employees, despite a federal regulation requiring them to provide such coverage).

28–29   **decision to uphold President Trump's travel ban:** *Trump v. Hawaii*, 138 S.Ct. 2392, 2433 (2018) (Sotomayor, J., dissenting) (criticizing the Court for upholding "a policy first advertised openly and unequivocally as a 'total and complete shutdown of Muslims entering the United States' because the policy now masquerades behind a facade of national-security concerns").

29   **including the right to an abortion:** *June Med. Servs. L.L.C. v. Russo*, 207 L. Ed. 2d 566, 574 (2020).

29   **the right to be free from anti-LGBTQ discrimination:** *Bostock v. Clayton Cty.*, 207 L. Ed. 2d 218, 230 (2020).

29   **the right to an abortion is unlikely to survive much longer:** See Ian Millhiser, "Why Conservative Chief Justice Roberts Just Struck Down an Anti-Abortion Law," Vox, June 29, 2020, at https://www.vox.com/2020/6/29/21306895/supreme-court-abortion-chief-justice-john-roberts-stephen-breyer-june-medical-russo ("The best reading of the Court's decision in *June Medical Services v. Russo* is that Roberts just gave the constitutional right to an abortion a potentially very brief reprieve. And he did so largely because Louisiana presented the weakest possible case in *June Medical*.")

CHAPTER ONE

31   **the state's "monster" voter suppression law:** William Wan, "Inside the Republican Creation of the North Carolina Voting Bill Dubbed the 'Monster' Law," *Washington Post*, September 2, 2016, at https://www.washingtonpost.com/politics/courts_law/inside-the-republican-creation-of-the-north-carolina-voting-bill-dubbed-the-monster-law/2016/09/01/79162398-6adf-11e6-8225-fbb8a6fc65bc_story.html.

31   **all of which disproportionately affected African Americans:** *N.C. State Conf. of the NAACP v. McCrory*, 831 F.3d 204, 214 (4th Cir. 2016).

31   **"requested data on the use, by race, of a number of voting practices.":** *N.C. State Conf. of the NAACP v. McCrory*, 831 F.3d 204, 214

31   **a problem, in-person voter fraud at the polls, that is virtually nonexistent:** Ian Millhiser, "Voting Rights Advocates Just Won a Small

but Important Victory in Missouri," Vox, January 16, 2020, at https://www.vox.com/2020/1/16/21067110/missouri-voter-id-supreme-court-priorities-usa-state.

32 **also prohibited voters from using certain forms of government-issued identification:** *N.C. State Conf. of the NAACP v. McCrory*, 182 F. Supp. 3d 320, 496 (M.D.N.C. 2016).

32 **"only those types of photo ID disproportionately held by whites":** *McCrory*, 831 F.3d at 227.

32 **over 64 percent of African Americans voted early:** *McCrory*, 831 F.3d at 216.

32 **eliminated one of the two Sunday voting days:** *McCrory*, 831 F.3d at 216–17.

32 **Republican governor Pat McCrory signed this law in August of 2013:** Aaron Blake, "North Carolina Governor Signs Extensive Voter ID Law," *Washington Post*, August 12, 2013.

32 **Republican leader announced plans to enact an "omnibus" election law:** *McCrory*, 831 F.3d at 214.

33 **CNN exit polls found that:** "Exit polls," CNN, November 15, 2016, at https://www.cnn.com/election/2016/results/exit-polls/north-carolina/president.

33 **race for the governor's mansion was decided by fewer than five thousand votes:** "2016 North Carolina Governor Election Results," *Politico*, December 13, 2016, at https://www.politico.com/2016-election/results/map/governor/north-carolina/.

33 **NBC exit polls still show:** "Exit Polls 2020," NBC News (last visited November 9, 2020) at https://www.nbcnews.com/politics/2020-elections/exit-polls.

33 **the Court's Republicans voted to reinstate nearly all of the law in 2016:** *North Carolina v. N.C. State Conf. of the NAACP*, 137 S. Ct. 27, 28 (2016).

33 **targets "African Americans with almost surgical precision":** *McCrory*, 831 F.3d at 214.

34 **it is likely that the Court now has the votes to destroy the fourth:** Ian Millhiser, "Let's Think About Court-Packing," *Democracy: A Journal of Ideas* (2019) at https://democracyjournal.org/magazine/51/lets-think-about-court-packing-2/.

34 **In *Crawford v. Marion County Election Board*:** 533 U.S. 181 (2008).

34 **found just thirty-five credible allegations:** German Lopez, "The Case Against Voter ID laws, in One Chart," Vox, August 6, 2015, at https://www.vox.com/2015/8/6/9107927/voter-id-election-fraud.

126   34   **none of which were the kind that could be prevented:** Ian Millhiser, "BREAKING: Texas' Voter ID Law Struck Down by an Extraordinarily Conservative Appeals Court," Think Progress, July 20, 2016, at https://thinkprogress.org/breaking-texas-voter-id-law-struck-down-by-an-extraordinarily-conservative-appeals-court-48bc0293f55b/.

34   **found zero cases of voter impersonation:** Josh Israel, "Iowa's Republican Secretary of State Just Proved That Voter ID Laws Are Unnecessary," Think Progress, May 9, 2014, at https://thinkprogress.org/iowas-republican-secretary-of-state-just-proved-that-voter-id-laws-are-unnecessary-cdb0729ff3b4/.

34   **was only able to identify a single case of in-person voter fraud:** *Crawford*, 533 U.S. at 1619 n. 12.

35   **estimated that a Pennsylvania voter ID law would have reduced:** Ian Millhiser, "Voting Rights Advocates Just Won a Small but Important Victory in Missouri."

36   **more voting machines to polling places in white neighborhoods:** Nicole Narea, "Black and Latino Voters Were Hit Hardest by Long Lines in the Texas Democratic Primary," Vox, March 3, 2020, at https://www.vox.com/2020/3/3/21164014 /long-lines-wait-texas-primary-democratic-harris.

36   **should not have an excessively complicated voter registration process:** See Ian Millhiser, "Georgia Republicans' Constitutionally Dubious Attempt to Cancel a State Election, Explained," Vox, March 16, 2020, at https://www.vox.com/2020/3/16/21178993/georgia-republicans-cancel-election-brian-kemp-john-barrow ("[I]f a hypothetical voter was listed as 'Tyrone Williams-Smith' on a voter registration form, and 'Tyrone Williams Smith' [without a hyphen] in the state's driver services records, that could be enough to deny this person the right to vote.").

36   **as the Supreme Court held in** *Burdick v. Takushi:* 504 U.S. 428 (1992).

36   **"A court considering a challenge to a state election law must weigh":** 504 U.S. 434.

37   **the proposed change would not be approved if it had:** *Shelby County v. Holder*, 133 S.Ct. 2612, 2634 (2013) (quoting 42 U.S.C. § 1973c(a)).

37   **southern states could lock African Americans out of the polls:** Ian Millhiser, *Injustices*, 185–87.

37   **states frequently run two, three, or even four elections:** Ian

Millhiser, "The Supreme Court Just Made It Easier to Get Away with Gerrymandering," Think Progress, June 5, 2017, at https: //thinkprogress.org/supreme -court-easier-gerrymandering -e6c986056e62/.

38 **On the day President Lyndon Johnson signed this act into law:** Ian Millhiser, "How Conservatives Abandoned Judicial Restraint, Took Over the Courts And Radically Transformed America," 192.

38 **Texas announced that its voter ID law and its racially gerrymandered legislative maps:** Aviva Shen, "Two Hours After the Supreme Court Gutted the Voting Rights Act, Texas AG Suppresses Minority Voters," Think Progress, June 25, 2013.

38 **is a tribute to wishful thinking:** *Shelby County*, 133 S.Ct. at 2641.

38 **"[T]hings have changed dramatically," Roberts wrote:** *Shelby County*, 133 S.Ct. at 2625.

38 **simply isn't racist enough anymore to justify:** *Shelby County*, 133 S.Ct. at 2618.

38 **empirical studies have shown that "racial resentment":** German Lopez, "The Past Year of Research Has Made It Very Clear: Trump Won Because of Racial Resentment," Vox, December 15,

2017, at https://www.vox.com /identities/2017/12/15/16781222 /trump-racism-economic-anxiety -study.

39 **"is like throwing away your umbrella in a rainstorm":** *Shelby County*, 133 S.Ct. at 2650 (Ginsburg, J., dissenting).

39 **left much of the Voting Rights Act intact:** 52 U.S.C. § 10301.

40 **2018 exit polls show that:** "Exit polls," CNN (last visited April 11, 2020) at https://www.cnn.com /election/2018/exit-polls.

40 **Except that, in *Abbott v. Perez*:** 138 S.Ct. 2305 (2018).

40–41 **were eventually stuck down as illegal racial gerrymanders:** 138 S.Ct. 2317.

41 **The full 2011 map never took effect:** 138 S.Ct. 2316.

41 **it wasn't relieving Texas of its obligation to draw legal maps:** Ian Millhiser, "Supreme Court Just Wrote a Presumption of White Racial Innocence into the Constitution," Think Progress, June 25, 2018, at https://archive .thinkprogress.org/scotus -presumption-of-white-racial -innocence-gerrymandering -7ad4fdfc82a5/.

42 **enjoy an extraordinarily high presumption of racial innocence:** *Perez*, 138 S.Ct. at 2324.

42 **"the only direct evidence brought to our attention":** *Perez*, 138 S.Ct. at 2327.

43 **term that it could use to weaken, or even destroy outright, the results test:** Ian Millhiser, "The Supreme Court Will Hear a Case That Could Destroy What Remains of the Voting Rights Act," Vox, October 2, 2020, at https://www.vox.com/2020/10/2/21498587/supreme-court-voting-rights-act-amy-coney-barrett.

43 **the Supreme Court's decision in *City of Mobile v. Bolden*:** 446 U.S. 55 (1980).

43 **this allowed the city's white majority to vote as a bloc:** 446 U.S. at 97–98 (White, J., dissenting).

43 **voting rights plaintiffs must show that a law was enacted with a "racially discriminatory motivation":** 446 U.S. at 62 (plurality opinion).

44 **over the strenuous objection of a young Justice Department attorney named John Roberts:** Ian Millhiser, "If Kavanaugh Is Confirmed, You Can Kiss the Right to Vote Goodbye," Think Progress, July 16, 2018, at https://archive.thinkprogress.org/the-supreme-court-and-the-coming-voting-rights-apocalypse-f0f0b2a069d1/.

44 **he found his new employer to be such an exciting place:** Ari Berman, "Inside John Roberts' Decades-Long Crusade Against the Voting Rights Act," *Politico*, August 10, 2015, at https://www.politico.com/magazine/story/2015/08/john-roberts-voting-rights-act-121222.

44 **Roberts became the Reagan administration's point person:** Ari Berman, "Inside John Roberts' Decades-Long Crusade Against the Voting Rights Act."

44 **"required States to obtain federal permission before enacting any law related to voting":** *Shelby County v. Holder*, 133 S. Ct. 2612, 2618 (2013).

45 **the younger John Roberts wrote in a memo arguing against the results test:** Ari Berman, "Inside John Roberts' Decades-Long Crusade Against the Voting Rights Act."

45 **proposed amendment to the Voting Rights Act would violate the Constitution itself:** Ian Millhiser, "If Kavanaugh Is Confirmed, You Can Kiss the Right to Vote Goodbye."

45 **Justice Lewis Powell used in *Regents of the University of California v. Bakke*:** 438 U.S. 265 (1978).

45 **when he struck down a medical school's affirmative action program:** 438 U.S. at 289.

45 **racial conservatives have used the word "quota":**

Ian Millhiser, "Supreme Court Just Wrote a Presumption of White Racial Innocence into the Constitution."

45   heard *Texas Department of Housing and Community Affairs v. Inclusive Communities Project*: 135 S. Ct. 2507 (2015).

45   asked whether the Fair Housing Act permits "disparate impact" lawsuits: 135 S. Ct. at 2513 (quoting *Ricci v. DeStefano*, 557 U.S. 557, 577 (2009)).

46   "the way to stop discrimination on the basis of race": *Parents Involved in Cmty. Sch. v. Seattle Sch. Dist. No. 1*, 551 U.S. 701, 748 (2007) (plurality opinion of Roberts, C.J.).

46   he saw a similar problem: Transcript of Oral Argument at 30, *Texas Dep't of Housing and Community Affairs v. Inclusive Communities Project*, 135 S. Ct. 2507 (2014) (No. 13-1371).

47   could have potentially disenfranchised thousands of African Americans: Alice Miranda Ollstein, "After Alabama Enforces Voter ID, Shuts Down DMVs in Black Communities, Lawmaker Wants Investigation," Think Progress, October 6, 2015, at https://thinkprogress.org /after-alabama-enforces-voter -id-shuts-down-dmvs-in-black -communities-lawmaker-wants -investigation-94de2c4a5dd9/.

47   after an Obama administration probe determined: "Feds: Alabama to Expand Driver's License Office Hours After Probe," Associated Press, December 28, 2016, at https://www.al.com /news/montgomery/2016/12/feds _alabama_to_expand_drivers.html.

47   cast a ballot in a polling place located at an historically Black college: Ari Berman, "Here's Why Texans Had to Wait Six Hours to Vote," *Mother Jones*, March 4, 2020, at https://www.motherjones .com/politics/2020/03 /texas-primary-lines/.

48   was just one of countless voters in heavily Democratic Houston: Ari Berman, "Here's Why Texans Had to Wait Six Hours to Vote."

48   was not an isolated incident: Ari Berman, "Here's Why Texans Had to Wait Six Hours to Vote."

48   According to the *Guardian*'s Richard Salame: Richard Salame, "Texas Closes Hundreds of Polling Sites, Making It Harder for Minorities to Vote," The Guardian, March 2, 2020, at https://www .theguardian.com/us-news/2020 /mar/02/texas-polling-sites -closures-voting.

49   an equally aggressive effort to maximize Democratic representation in Maryland: *Rucho v. Common Cause*, 139 S.Ct. 2484, 2491 (2019).

130

49 **In Michigan, Obama won by nearly ten points:** Ian Millhiser, "The Cracks in the GOP's Gerrymandering Firewall," Vox, September 11, 2019, at https://www.vox.com/policy-and-politics/2019/9/11/20857934/republican-gerrymandering-north-carolina-michigan.

50 **but many of them remained potent years later:** Ian Millhiser, "Wisconsin's Supreme Court Rules Along Partisan Lines to Require the State to Hold Its Election on Tuesday," Vox, April 6, 2020, at https://www.vox.com/2020/4/6/21209670/wisconsin-governor-delays-election-tony-evers-republicans-state-supreme-court.

50 **Justice Elena Kagan wrote in** *Rucho v. Common Cause:* 139 S.Ct. 2484 (2019).

50 **"partisan gerrymanders subject certain voters to 'disfavored treatment'":** 139 S.Ct. at 2514 (Kagan, J., dissenting).

50 **federal courts are not even permitted to consider cases challenging partisan gerrymanders:** 139 S.Ct. at 2506–07.

51 **upheld Arizona's redistricting commission in** *Arizona State Legislature v. Arizona Independent Redistricting Commission:* 576 U.S. 787 (2015).

51 **"the Times, Places, and Manner of holding Elections for Senators and Representatives":** U.S. Const., § 4, cl. 1.

51 **a state may determine how it will conduct federal elections:** *Ariz. State Legis.,* 576 U.S. at 808.

52 **began agitating for a different reading of the word "Legislature":** *Democratic Nat'l Comm. v. Wis. State Legis.,* 2020 U.S. LEXIS 5187, at *4 (October 26, 2020) (Gorsuch, J., concurring).

CHAPTER TWO

53 **the Supreme Court handed down an unexpected order:** *West Virginia v. EPA,* 136 S.Ct. 1000, 1000 (2016) (internal citations omitted).

53 **was expected to reduce overall carbon dioxide emissions:** Environmental Protection Agency, Carbon Pollution Emission Guidelines for Existing Stationary Sources: Electric Utility Generating Units, 80 Fed. Reg. 64,662, 64,665 (Oct. 23, 2015) (hereinafter "Clean Power Plan").

53 **That's the equivalent of removing 166 million cars:** "FACT SHEET: Clean Power Plan by the Numbers," Environmental Protection Agency, https://archive.epa.gov/epa/cleanpowerplan/fact-sheet-clean-power-plan-numbers.html (last visited Mar. 22, 2020).

54   "public health and climate benefits worth an estimated $34 billion to $54 billion": "FACT SHEET: Clean Power Plan by the Numbers."

54   replaced this Obama-era policy with a significantly weaker rule: Umair Irfan, "Trump's EPA Just Replaced Obama's Signature Climate Policy with a Much Weaker Rule," Vox, June 19, 2019, at https://www .vox.com/2019/6/19/18684054 /climate-change-clean-power-plan -repeal-affordable-emissions.

54   "deconstruction of the administrative state": Phillip Rucker and Robert Costa, "Bannon Vows a Daily Fight for 'Deconstruction of the Administrative State,'" Washington Post, February 23, 2017, at https://www .washingtonpost.com/politics /top-wh-strategist-vows-a -daily-fight-for-deconstruction -of-the-administrative-state /2017/02/23/03f6b8da-f9ea-11e6 -bf01-d47f8cf9b643_story.html.

55   used it to bar doctors from discriminating against transgender patients: Ian Lovett and Louise Radnofsky, "U.S. Sued over New Transgender Health-Care Protections," Wall Street Journal, August 24, 2016, at https://www.wsj.com/articles /u-s-sued-over-new-transgender -health-care-regulation -1471995720.

55   pushed to expand overtime pay to approximately 1.3 million workers: Alexia Fernández Campbell, "1.3 Million Winners and 2.8 Million Losers from Trump's New Overtime Rule," Vox, September 24, 2019, at https://www.vox.com /identities/2019/9/24/20835653 /trump-overtime-pay-rule -explained.

55   required most health plans to cover a wide range of treatments: Burwell v. Hobby Lobby Stores, 134 S.Ct. 2751, 2762 (2014).

55   proposed rules weakening the ban on sexual harassment on campus: Department of Education, Nondiscrimination on the Basis of Sex in Education Programs or Activities Receiving Federal Financial Assistance, 83 Fed. Reg. 61462 (November 29, 2018).

55   diluting the federal ban on housing discrimination: Department of Housing and Urban Development, HUD's Implementation of the Fair Housing Act's Disparate Impact Standard, 84 Fed. Reg. 42854 (October 18, 2019).

55   104 different regulations seeking to protect the environment: Nadja Popovich, et al, "95 Environmental Rules Being Rolled Back Under Trump," New York Times, December 21, 2019, at https://www.nytimes.com /interactive/2019/climate/trump -environment-rollbacks.html.

132   56   **federal immigration law "exudes deference to the President:** *Trump v. Hawaii*, 138 S.Ct. 2392, 2408 (2018).

56   **a policy restricting transgender individuals from serving in the military:** *Trump v. Stockman*, 139 S.Ct. 950, 950 (2019).

56   **strict limits on immigrants seeking asylum:** *Barr v. East Bay Sanctuary Covenant*, 140 S.Ct. 3, 4 (2019) (Sotomayor, J., dissenting).

56   **restrictions on low-income immigrants:** *Wolf v. Cook County*, 140 S.Ct. 681, 681–82 (2020) (Sotomayor, J., dissenting).

56   **"putting a thumb on the scale" in favor of that administration:** 140 S.Ct. at 684 (Sotomayor, J, dissenting).

57   **rules governing power plants could evolve as technology improves:** 42 U.S.C. § 7411(a)(1).

57   **the job of figuring out what the "best system of emission reduction" is:** 42 U.S.C. § 7411(a)(1).

57   **to achieve the "best system of emission reduction":** Clean Power Plan, 80 Fed. Reg. 64, 666–67.

58   **two foundational Supreme Court decisions preserving agencies' ability:** *Gutierrez-Brizuela v. Lynch*, 834 F. 3d 1142,

1149 (10th Cir. 2016) (Gorsuch, J., concurring).

58   **Gorsuch called for strict new limits on the federal government's power to regulate:** See *Gundy v. United States*, 139 S.Ct. 2116, 2135–37 (2019) (Gorusch, J., dissenting) (suggesting new limits on the executive branch's regulatory authority).

58   **they agree with Gorsuch's plans to restrict agency power:** Ian Millhiser, "Brett Kavanaugh's Latest Opinion Should Terrify Democrats," Vox, November 26, 2019, at https://www.vox .com/2019/11/26/20981758/brett -kavanaughs-terrify-democrats -supreme-court-gundy-paul.

59   **"Broad delegation to the Executive is the hallmark of the modern administrative state":** Antonin Scalia, "Judicial Deference to Administrative Interpretations of Law," *Duke L.J.* 1989, 511, 516.

59   **he saw these shifting approaches as a positive thing:** Antonin Scalia, "Judicial Deference to Administrative Interpretations of Law," 518.

59   **limiting the judiciary's power to second-guess federal agencies:** 467 U.S. 837 (1984).

60   **courts generally should defer to the agency's interpretation:** 467 U.S. at 843.

60   **such deference to agencies is warranted for two reasons:** 467 U.S. at 865.

60   **it is better to leave these discretionary judgments to government officials:** 467 U.S. at 865–66.

61   **"In the long run *Chevron* will endure," he predicted:** Antonin Scalia, "Judicial Deference to Administrative Interpretations of Law," 521.

61   **this case, *Gutierrez-Brizuela v. Lynch*:** 834 F.3d 1142 (10th Cir. 2016).

61   **where Gorsuch labeled the federal administrative state a "behemoth":** 834 F.3d at 1149 (Gorsuch, J., concurring).

62   **it is better to give judges the final word on regulations:** 834 F.3d at 1153 (Gorsuch, J., concurring).

63   **they expected him to take a narrow view of federal agencies' power to regulate:** David A. Kaplan, *The Most Dangerous Branch*, 42.

63   **who would go on to become a finalist for the Supreme Court:** See Tinsley E. Yarbrough, *David Hackett Souter* (2005), 103 (identifying Starr as one of five candidates President George H. W. Bush considered for the Supreme Court vacancy in 1990).

63–64   **it allowed political actors to reshape regulations:** Kenneth

W. Starr, "Judicial Review in the Post-Chevron Era," 3 *Yale J. on Reg.* 283 (1986), 312.

64   **"I believe they have a duty voluntarily to exercise 'judicial restraint.'":** Kenneth W. Starr, "Judicial Review in the Post-Chevron Era," 308.

64   **President Reagan had an astounding 68 percent approval rating:** "Reagan's Approval Rating Is Highest Yet, Gallup Poll Finds," *New York Times*, June 15, 1986, at https://www.nytimes.com /1986/06/15/us/reagan-s-approval -rating-is-highest-yet-gallup -poll-finds.html.

65   **gives tiny red states like Wyoming exactly the same number of senators:** Ian Millhiser, "America's Anti-Democratic Senate, by the Numbers," Vox, November 6, 2020, at https://www .vox.com/2020/11/6/21550979 /senate-malapportionment-20 -million-democrats-republicans -supreme-court.

65   **Democratic senators represent more than forty million more people:** Ian Millhiser, "America's Anti-Democratic Senate, by the Numbers."

66   **first of these two cases is *Kisor v. Wilkie*:** 139 S.Ct. 2400 (2019).

66   **after the Supreme Court's decision in *Auer v. Robbins*:** 591 U.S. 452 (1997).

134

66 requires courts to defer to "agencies' reasonable readings": *Kisor*, 139 S.Ct. at 2408.

66 conservative justices arguing that *Auer* should be abandoned: See *Kisor*, 139 S.Ct. at 2437 (Gorsuch, J., concurring in the judgment) ("Not only is *Auer* incompatible with the APA; it also sits uneasily with the Constitution.")

66 warning that courts should be hesitant to apply *Auer*: See *Kisor*, 139 S.Ct. at 2414 ("*Auer* deference is not the answer to every question of interpreting an agency's rules. Far from it. As we explain in this section, the possibility of deference can arise only if a regulation is genuinely ambiguous.")

66 "the rule of law begins to bleed into the rule of men": *Kisor*, 139 S.Ct. at 2438 (Gorsuch, J., concurring in the judgment).

67 "are not, nor are they supposed to be, 'wholly impartial.'": *Kisor v. Wilkie*, 139 S.Ct. 2400, 2438–39 (2019) (Gorsuch, J., concurring in the judgment).

67 "their own interests, their own constituencies, and their own policy goals": *Kisor*, 139 S.Ct. at 2439.

67 decision in *Department of Commerce v. New York*: 139 S.Ct. 2551 (2019).

67 "counting the whole number of persons in each state": U.S. Const., Amend. XIV.

68 would lead to a "5.1 percent decline in response rates": *New York*, 139 S.Ct. at 2571.

68 "could seriously jeopardize the accuracy of the census": Ian Millhiser, "This SCOTUS Case Will Reveal How Willing Chief Justice Roberts Is to Politicize the Court," Think Progress, April 16, 2019, at https://archive.thinkprogress .org/supreme-court-case-chief -justice-roberts-voting-rights -1b8f7f865306/.

68 "clearly be a disadvantage to the Democrats": Ian Millhiser, "Justice Alito's Jurisprudence of White Racial Innocence," Vox, April 23, 2020, at https://www .vox.com/2020/4/23/21228636 /alito-racism-ramos-louisiana -unanimous-jury.

68 claimed that he planned to add the citizenship question: *New York*, 139 S.Ct. at 2563.

68 didn't show much interest in Voting Rights Act enforcement: Ian Millhiser, "DOJ's Civil Rights Division Has Not Filed a Single Voting Rights Act Case Since Trump Took Office," Think Progress, November 5, 2018, at https://archive.thinkprogress.org /civil-rights-division-has -not-filed-a-single-voting

-rights-act-case-under-trump
-792914a2689a/.

68 **hasn't asked a citizenship question on its main form since 1950:** *New York*, 139 S.Ct. at 2556.

69 **evidence showed that the Secretary was determined:** *New York*, 139 S.Ct. at 2574.

69 **"rested on a pretextual basis":** *New York*, 139 S.Ct. at 2573.

70 **"reflects an unprecedented departure from our deferential review":** *New York*, 139 S.Ct. at 2576 (Thomas, J., dissenting).

70 **could be tied up in an "endless morass of discovery and policy disputes":** *New York*, 139 S.Ct. (Thomas, J, dissenting).

70 **"that a judge predisposed to distrust the Secretary":** *New York*, 139 S.Ct. at 2582 (Thomas, J., dissenting).

72 **The Constitution gives Congress the "legislative" power:** U.S. Const. Art. I § 1.

72 **president and the various federal agencies that answer to the president the "executive" power:** U.S. Const. at Art. II § 1.

72 **"adopt generally applicable rules of conduct governing future actions":** *Gundy v. United States*, 139 S.Ct. 2116, 2134 (2019).

73 **quote a passage from the political philosopher John**

Locke: *Gundy v. United States*, 139   135
S.Ct. (quoting John Locke, *Second Treatise of Government* § 141 (Thomas Hollis ed. 1764)).

73 **Locke raised no objection to a legislature delegating a power:** Julian Davis Mortenson and Nicholas Bagley, Delegation at the Founding (U. of Michigan Public Law Research Paper No. 658), 32 at https://papers.ssrn.com/sol3 /papers.cfm?abstract_id=3512154.

73 **"a delegated power from the people":** Julian Davis Mortenson and Nicholas Bagley, Delegation at the Founding, 27 ("For the founders . . . government's very existence meant that the 'original legislative power' had already been delegated.")

74 **enacted numerous laws giving vast discretion to other government officials:** Julian Davis Mortenson and Nicholas Bagley, Delegation at the Founding, 71 (quoting Act of August 7, 1789, 1 Stat. 50, 50-51).

74 **so long as they "deem the invention or discovery sufficiently useful or important":** Julian Davis Mortenson and Nicholas Bagley, Delegation at the Founding, 75 (quoting Act of April 10, 1790, 1 Stat. 109, 110 (first Patent Act)).

74 **would govern license holders "in all things touching the said trade and intercourse.":** Julian Davis Mortenson and

136   Nicholas Bagley, Delegation at the Founding, 78.

74   **allowed the president to identify wounded or disabled soldiers:** Julian Davis Mortenson and Nicholas Bagley, Delegation at the Founding, 80 (quoting Act of April 30, 1790, 1 Stat. 119, 121).

74   **power to grant citizenship to any free white person:** Julian Davis Mortenson and Nicholas Bagley, Delegation at the Founding, 86 (quoting Act of March 26, 1790, 1 Stat. 103).

75   **As the Court explained in *Mistretta v. United States*:** 488 U.S. 361 (1989).

75   **absent an ability to delegate power:** 488 U.S. at 372.

75   **Congress may delegate regulatory power to agencies:** 488 U.S. 372 (quoting J. W. Hampton, Jr., Co. v. United States, 276 U.S. 394, 409 (1928)).

75   **eight remaining justices heard *Gundy v. United States*:** 139 S.Ct. 2116 (2019).

75   **argued that Congress did not lawfully delegate:** *Gundy*, 139 S.Ct. at 2122.

76   **delegations of power to agencies must be struck down:** *Gundy*, 139 S.Ct. at 2133, 2136.

77   **In *Little Sisters v. Pennsylvania*:** 140 S.Ct. 2367 (2020).

77   **agency determined that contraceptive care must be covered:** 140 S.Ct. at 2370.

77   **"virtually unbridled discretion to decide what counts as preventive care and screenings":** 140 S.Ct. at 2380.

77   **may strike down other, similarly worded provisions of Obamacare:** Ian Millhiser, "The Supreme Court Just Gave Republicans a Powerful New Weapon Against Obamacare," Vox, July 8, 2020, at https://www .vox.com/2020/7/8/21317323 /supreme-court-obamacare -little-sisters-clarence-thomas -pennsylvania-birth-control.

77   **have both signaled in other opinions:** See id. at 2131 (Alito, J., concurring in the judgment) ("If a majority of this Court were willing to reconsider the approach we have taken for the past 84 years, I would support that effort."); *Paul v. United States*, 140 S.Ct. 342, 342 (Statement of Kavanaugh, J.) ("Justice Gorsuch's scholarly analysis of the Constitution's nondelegation doctrine in his *Gundy* dissent may warrant further consideration in future cases.")

78   **judges "are not part of either political branch":** *Chevron USA Inc. v. Natural Resources Defense Council, Inc.*, 467 US 837, 865–66 (1984).

CHAPTER THREE

79 **lost those customers after they learned about Bessinger's peculiar ideology:** Kathleen Purvis, "Can a S.C. Barbecue Family Rise Above Their Father's History of Racism?" *Charlotte Observer*, December 8, 2016, at https://www.charlotteobserver.com/living/food-drink/article119660858.html.

79 **sold white supremacist tracts at his restaurants:** Kathleen Purvis, "Can a S.C. Barbecue Family Rise Above Their Father's History of Racism?"

79 **"blessed the Lord for allowing them to be enslaved and sent to America":** Ian Millhiser, "Why the Christian Right May Never Recover from Indiana," Think Progress, April 6, 2015, at https://archive.thinkprogress.org/why-the-christian-right-may-never-recover-from-indiana-19307ef3bb04/.

80 **claimed in a federal lawsuit, "contravenes the will of God":** *Newman v. Piggie Park Enterprises*, 390 U.S. 400, 402 n.5 (1968).

80 **Supreme Court that heard *Newman v. Piggie Park Enterprises*:** 390 U.S. 400 (1968).

80 **"is not even a borderline case":** 390 U.S. at 402 n.5.

80 **"in any marriage, the husband is the head of the household":** *EEOC v. Fremont Christian School* 781 F.3d 1362, 1364 (9th Cir. 1986).

80–81 **school typically did not offer health insurance to its married women employees:** 781 F.3d at 1364–65.

81 **"equally if not more compelling than other interests":** 781 F.3d at 1369.

81 **the right to "free exercise" of religion:** U.S. Const. Amend. I.

82 **the Roberts Court has moved the law significantly to the right:** See *Espinoza v. Montana Dept. of Revenue*, 140 S.Ct. 2246, 2261 (2020) ("A State need not subsidize private education. But once a State decides to do so, it cannot disqualify some private schools solely because they are religious."); *American Legion v. American Humanist Association*, 139 S.Ct. 2067, 2074 (2019) (upholding a massive, cross-shaped monument on government land).

82 **the Supreme Court warned nearly a century and a half ago:** *Reynolds v. United States*, 98 US 145, 167 (1879).

83 **begin with *Sherbert v. Verner*:** 374 U.S. 398 (1963).

83 **who refused to work on Saturday because that day is honored:** 374 U.S. at 399.

138   83   **sought unemployment benefits from the state of South Carolina:** 374 U.S. at 401.

83   **must advance "some compelling state interest":** 374 U.S. at 406.

84   **"precisely tailored to serve a compelling governmental interest":** *Fisher v. Univ. of Tex. at Austin* 570 U.S. 297, 308 (2013) (quoting *Univ. of Calif. v. Bakke*, 438 U.S. 265, 299 (1978) (opinion of Powell, J.)).

84   **may not use that objection to "abridge any other person's religious liberties.":** *Sherbert*, 374 U.S. at 409.

84   **thus gain a competitive advantage over other businesses:** *Tony & Susan Alamo Foundation v. Sec'y of Labor*, 471 U.S. 290, 303 (1985).

84   **But the data does not bear this claim out:** James E. Ryan, note, "Smith and the Religious Freedom Restoration Act: An Iconoclastic Assessment," *Va. L. Rev.* 78 (1992), 1407, 1417.

84   **indicates that a similar pattern continued into the next decade:** Adam Winkler, "Fatal in Theory and Strict in Fact: An Empirical Analysis of Strict Scrutiny in the Federal Courts," *Vanderbilt L. Rev.* 59 (2006), 793, 815.

85   **the Supreme Court decided** *Employment Division v. Smith*: 496 U.S. 913 (1990).

85   **had a constitutional right to practice one of their religious traditions:** 496 U.S. at 874–75.

85   **"does not relieve an individual of the obligation to comply":** 496 U.S. at 879 (quoting *United States v. Lee*, 455 U. S. 252, 263, n. 3 (1982) (STEVENS, J., concurring in judgment)).

86   **to enforce generally applicable prohibitions of socially harmful conduct:** 496 U.S. at 885.

86   **to "restore the compelling interest test":** 42 U.S.C. § 2000bb(b)(1).

86   **"the least restrictive means of furthering that compelling governmental interest.":** 42 U.S.C. § 2000bb–1(b).

87   **"the First Amendment was enacted precisely to protect the rights":** *Employment Div., Dept. of Human Resources of Ore. v. Smith*, 494 US 872, 902 (O'Connor, J. concurring in the judgment) (1990).

87   **"only to overturn the Supreme Court's decision in** *Smith*": *Burwell v. Hobby Lobby*, 134 S. Ct. 2751, 2791 (2014) (Ginsburg, J., dissenting) (quoting 139 Cong. Rec. 26178 (1993) (statement of Sen. Kennedy)).

87 "Congress expected courts considering RFRA claims": 134 S. Ct. (quoting S.Rep. No. 103-111, p. 8 (1993)).

88 is a perfect encapsulation of the Obama-era culture wars: 134 S.Ct. 2751 (2014).

88 requires most employee health plans to provide "'preventive care and screenings'": 134 S. Ct. at 2762 (quoting 42 U.S.C. § 300gg-13(a)(4)).

88 to include all forms of contraception: 134 S. Ct. at 2762

88 who (falsely) believed that four forms of birth control: See Jen Gunter, "The Medical Facts About Birth Control and Hobby Lobby—From an OB/GYN," New Republic, July 6, 2014, at https://newrepublic.com/article/118547/facts-about-birth-control-and-hobby-lobby-ob-gyn ("We can be very confident that three of the four contraceptives do not lead to abortion, even using the conservative definition of when life begins, and we can be almost [although not quite] as sure that the fourth does not, either.")

88 are abortifacients and thus conflict with their religious objections: Hobby Lobby, 134 S.Ct. at 2765.

89 RFRA limits the government's ability to: 42 U.S.C. § 2000bb-1(b).

89 RFRA defined the term "exercise of religion": Hobby Lobby, 134 S.Ct. at 2761 (quoting § 2000bb-2(4) (1994 ed.)).

89 "an obvious effort to effect a complete separation from First Amendment case law": 134 S.Ct. (quoting § 2000cc-5(7)(A)).

89 amended RFRA statute still states that the purpose of RFRA: 42 U.S.C. § 2000bb(b)(1) (internal citations omitted).

90 that they typically apply to laws that discriminate: Hobby Lobby, 134 S.Ct. at 2780.

90 In City of Boerne v. Flores: 521 U.S. 507 (1997).

90 RFRA does not apply to state laws that burden religious practice: See 521 U.S. at 533 ("The stringent test RFRA demands of state laws reflects a lack of proportionality or congruence between the means adopted and the legitimate end to be achieved.")

90 may grant exemptions to people with religious objections to anti-discrimination laws: Hobby Lobby, 134 S.Ct. at 2804–05 (Ginsburg, J., dissenting).

90 Masterpiece Cakeshop v. Colorado Civil Rights Commission: 138 S.Ct. 1719 (2018).

90 who refused to make a wedding cake for a gay couple: 138 S.Ct. at 1724.

91   **the baker claimed that requiring him to obey:** 138 S.Ct. at 1726.

91   **Kennedy gave Phillips a very narrow victory:** 138 S.Ct. at 1729.

91   **has been used to justify all kinds of discrimination throughout history:** 138 S.Ct. at 1729.

91   **theologians argued that slavery was an act of providence:** Julie Zauzmer, "The Bible Was Used to Justify Slavery. Then Africans Made It Their Path to Freedom," *Washington Post,* April 30, 2019, at https://www.washingtonpost .com/local/the-bible-was -used-to-justify-slavery-then -africans-made-it-their-path-to -freedom/2019/04/29/34699e8e -6512-11e9-82ba-fcfeff232e8f _story.html.

92   **In *Loving v. Virginia*:** 388 U.S. 1 (1967).

92   **"Almighty God created the races white, black, yellow, malay and red":** 388 U.S. at 3.

92   **deemed the Colorado civil rights commissioner's statement:** *Masterpiece Cakeshop, Ltd. v. Colo. Civil Rights Comm'n,* 138 S.Ct. 1719, 1729 (2018).

92   **"it is unexceptional that Colorado law can protect gay persons" from discrimination:** 138 S.Ct. at 1728.

93   **A merchant may refuse to sell a particular product altogether:** 138 S.Ct. at 1732 (Kagan, J., concurring).

93   **is alone "entitled to define the nature of his religious commitments":** 138 S.Ct. at 1739 (Gorsuch, J., concurring).

94   **CSS refuses to place foster children with a same-sex couple:** *Fulton v. City of Philadelphia,* 922 F. 3d 140, 147–48 (3d. Cir. 2019).

94   **violated CSS's contract with the city, which forbids discrimination:** 922 F. 3d at 148.

94   **even if it insists on discriminating against some residents:** 922 F. 3d at 152.

95   **Alito offered a narrow caveat to his opinion:** *Burwell v. Hobby Lobby Stores,* Inc., 134 S. Ct. 2751, 2783 (2014).

96   **the Supreme Court may allow religious objectors to undercut:** *United States v. Lee,* 455 U.S. 252, 254–55 (1982).

96   **Or consider *Tony & Susan Alamo Foundation v. Secretary of Labor*:** 471 U.S. 290 (1985).

96   **whether an employer may seek a religious objection to minimum wage laws:** 471 U.S. at 291–92.

97   **"untenable to allow individuals to seek exemptions from taxes":** 134 S.Ct at 2764.

CHAPTER FOUR

98 **underlying dispute in *AT&T Mobility v. Concepcion*:** 563 U.S. 333 (2011).

98 **they were actually charged $30.22 in sales tax:** 563 U.S. at 337.

99 **"give the merchants the right or the privilege of sitting down":** *Gilmer v. Interstate/Johnson Lane Corp.*, 500 U.S. 20, 39 (1991) (Stevens, J., dissenting) (quoting Hearing on S. 4213 and S. 4214 before a Subcommittee of the Senate Committee on the Judiciary, 67th Cong., 4th Sess., 9 (1923)).

99 **which looked at forced arbitration in employment cases:** Katherine V. W. Stone and Alexander J. S. Colvin, "The Arbitration Epidemic: Mandatory Arbitration Deprives Workers and Consumers of Their Rights," Economic Policy Institute, December 7, 2015, 19, at https://files.epi.org/2015/arbitration-epidemic.pdf.

100 **specifically exempts "workers engaged in foreign or interstate commerce":** 9 U.S.C. § 1.

100 **yet, in *Circuit City v. Adams*:** 532 U.S. 105 (2001).

100 **forced arbitration agreements may be enforced:** 532 U.S. at 109.

100 **companies may insert a ban on class action lawsuits:** See *AT&T Mobility LLC v. Concepcion*,

563 U.S. 333, 346–47 (2011) (holding that a prohibition on contracts banning class actions "interferes with arbitration").

101 **"the *realistic* alternative to a class action is not 17 million individual suits":** *Carnegie v. Household Intern., Inc.*, 376 F. 3d 656, 661 (2004).

101 **often emphasize that courts must apply:** *Moses H. Cone Memorial Hospital v. Mercury Construction Corp.*, 460 U.S. 1, 24 (1983).

102 **a worker who refuses to sign away their right to sue:** See *Epic Sys. Corp. v. Lewis*, 138 S. Ct. 1612, 1633 (2018) (Ginsburg, J., dissenting) ("[E]mployers required them to sign, as a condition of employment, arbitration agreements banning collective judicial and arbitral proceedings of any kind.")

102 ***Circuit City* turned on the meaning of a very important word:** *Circuit City v. Adams*, 532 U.S. 105, 111–12 (2001) (quoting 9 U. S. C. § 2) (emphasis added).

102 **"save upon such grounds as exist at law or in equity":** 9 U.S.C. § 2 (emphasis added).

102 **from this broader policy favoring arbitration contracts:** 532 U.S. at 109 (quoting 9 U. S. C. § 1) (emphasis added).

102 **its infamous child labor decision:** 247 U.S. 251, 272 (1918).

142

104   the word "commerce" must be read very broadly: *Circuit City*, 532 U.S. at 112.

104   yet, the Court also read the provision protecting: 532 U.S. at 109.

104   not how courts typically interpret laws: *Gustafson v. Alloyd Co.*, 513 US 561, 568 (1995).

105   does not prevent them from enforcing universal contracting laws: *AT&T Mobility LLC v. Concepcion*, 563 U.S. 333, 357 (Breyer, J., dissenting).

105   the right of companies to impose class action bans: In a decision that is widely mocked by conservatives, the Supreme Court held in *Griswold v. Connecticut*, 381 U.S. 479 (1965) that "specific guarantees in the Bill of Rights have penumbras, formed by emanations from those guarantees that help give them life and substance." Id. at 484.

105   a defendant who loses big in class arbitration typically has no way to appeal that decision: *Concepcion*, 563 U.S. at 348–50.

106   there must be a "federal policy favoring arbitration": 563 U.S. at 339 (quoting *Moses H. Cone Memorial Hospital v. Mercury Constr. Corp.*, 460 U.S. 1, 24 (1983)).

106   won rare praise from the civil rights community: *Bostock*

v. Clayton Cty., 207 L. Ed. 2d 218 (2020).

106   encompasses discrimination on the basis of sexual orientation: 207 L. Ed. 2d at 230.

106   is the Supreme Court's most outspoken evangelist of textualism: Neil Gorsuch, *A Republic, If You Can Keep It* (2019), 144.

106   did not believe that they were banning discrimination against LGBTQ Americans: Ian Millhiser, "The Supreme Court Showdown over LGBTQ Discrimination, Explained," Vox, October 8, 2019, at https://www.vox.com/2019/10/2/20883827/supreme-court-lgbtq-discrimination-title-vii-civil-rights-gay-trans-queer.

107   unavoidably encompasses discrimination against LGBTQ workers: *Bostock*, 207 L. Ed. at 234.

107   the employer intentionally penalizes a person: 207 L. Ed. 2d at 235.

107   his majority opinion in *Epic Systems v. Lewis*: 138 S.Ct. 1612 (2018).

107   to "sign, as a condition of employment, arbitration agreements": 138 S.Ct. at 1633 (Ginsburg, J., dissenting).

109 **Gorsuch's opinion begins with two rhetorical questions:** 138 S.Ct. at 1619.

109 **the entire purpose of the NLRA was to prevent employers:** 138 S.Ct. at 1634 (Ginsburg, J., dissenting).

109 **to "redress the bargaining power imbalance workers faced":** 138 S.Ct. at 1635 (Ginsburg, J., dissenting).

CONCLUSION

112 **to further weaken protections against racist voting laws:** Ian Millhiser, "The Supreme Court Will Hear a Case That Could Destroy What Remains of the Voting Rights Act," Vox, October 2, 2020, at https://www.vox.com /2020/10/2/21498587/supreme -court-voting-rights-act-amy -coney-barrett.

113 **they lost Congress's upper house because the Senate:** Matthew Yglesias, "American Democracy's Senate Problem, Explained," Vox, December 17, 2019, at https://www.vox.com/policy -and-politics/2019/12/17/21011079 /senate-bias-2020-data-for -progress.

113 **the GOP Senate that blocked Obama Supreme Court nominee:** Ian Millhiser, "A New Poll Shows Rank-and-File Democrats Finally Realize the Supreme Court Is Important," Vox, September 1, 2020, at https://www.vox.com /2020/9/1/21408512/poll-supreme -court-democrats-republicans -gap-merrick-garland.

Columbia Global Reports is a publishing imprint from Columbia University that commissions authors to do original on-site reporting around the globe on a wide range of issues. The resulting novella-length books offer new ways to look at and understand the world that can be read in a few hours. Most readers are curious and busy. Our books are for them.

Subscribe to Columbia Global Reports and get six books a year in the mail in advance of publication. globalreports.columbia.edu/subscribe

The Call: Inside the Global Saudi Religious Project
Krithika Varagur

The Socialist Awakening: What's Different Now About The Left
John B. Judis

Ghosting the News: Local Journalism and the Crisis of American Democracy
Margaret Sullivan

Carte Blanche: The Erosion of Medical Consent
Harriet A. Washington

Reading Our Minds: The Rise of Big Data Psychiatry
Daniel Barron

Freedomville: The Story of a 21st-Century Slave Revolt
Laura T. Murphy